THE W ATTITUDE ERA

Written by Jon Robinson

LEMEN BOYS AND GIRLS CH
PROUDLY BRINGS TO YOU
E ROAD DAWG JESSE JAMES
E NOT
DOWN WHERE
DOWN HERE!
Games 3:16
HEY CAMERAMAN

EDITORIAL MANAGER
Tim Fitzpatrick

BOOK DESIGNERS
Dan Caparo and Tim Amrhein

VP & PUBLISHER
Mike Degler

MARKETING MANAGER
Katie Hemlock

PROJECT EDITOR
Matt Buchanan

PRODUCTION DESIGNER
Wil Cruz

ASSOCIATE PUBLISHER
Andy Rolleri

DIGITAL PUBLISHING MANAGER
Tim Cox

SENIOR PROJECT EDITOR
Jennifer Sims

LICENSING MANAGER
Christian Sumner

OPERATIONS MANAGER
Stacey Beheler

DK/BradyGames, a division of Penguin Group (USA).
800 East 96th Street, 3rd Floor
Indianapolis, IN 46240

ISBN: 978-1-4654-3123-3

Printing Code: The rightmost double-digit number is the year of the book's printing; the rightmost single-digit number is the number of the book's printing. For example, 15-1 shows that the first printing of the book occurred in 2015.

18   17   16   15   4   3   2   1

Printed in China.

BradyGames sincerely thanks Steve Pantaleo, Josh Tottenham, and the rest of the amazing WWE team for all their help and support during this project.

Consumer Products
GLOBAL PUBLISHING MANAGER
Steve Pantaleo

SENIOR DIRECTOR, DOMESTIC LICENSING
Jess Richardson

SENIOR VICE PRESIDENT, GLOBAL LICENSING
Howard Brathwaite

EXECUTIVE VICE PRESIDENT, CONSUMER PRODUCTS
Casey Collins

Photo Department
Josh Tottenham, Frank Vitucci, Lea Riveccio, Jamie Nelson, Melissa Halladay, Mike Moran, and JD Sestito

Archives
ARCHIVIST
Ben Brown

Creative Services
SENIOR VICE PRESIDENT, CREATIVE SERVICES
Stan Stanski

CREATIVE DIRECTOR
John Jones

SENIOR ART DIRECTOR
Carla Leighton

Legal
VICE PRESIDENT, INTELLECTUAL PROPERTY
Lauren Dienes-Middlen

ABOUT THE AUTHOR

Jon Robinson is a writer/wrestling fanatic who has contributed to such publications as *ESPN The Magazine*, *ESPN.com*, *IGN* and *Sports Illustrated*. Past books include *Rumble Road* and *WWE: My Favorite Match*. Jon currently lives in the San Francisco Bay area with his wife and two children.

Thanks to WWE, my daughter skips around the house like AJ Lee, and my son wants to be the next Brock Lesnar. Luckily for me, I have a wife who is badder than any Diva out there to keep us all in line. Special thanks to Mike Archer, Steve Pantaleo, Tim Fitzpatrick, and the entire WWE/DK family for the time and access necessary to bring the Attitude Era back to life in book form—oh, hell yeah! Who knew that the connections I made back when I was writing about WWE video games as Johnny Ballgame for *GamePro Magazine* would come in handy all these years later? I was able to see the era from a unique point of view, hanging out backstage playing *Madden* against the likes of D-Lo Brown and The Rock. Those nights remain some of my favorite memories to this day.

Know your role, read the book, and hit me up on Twitter to let me know what you think: @JrobAndSteal

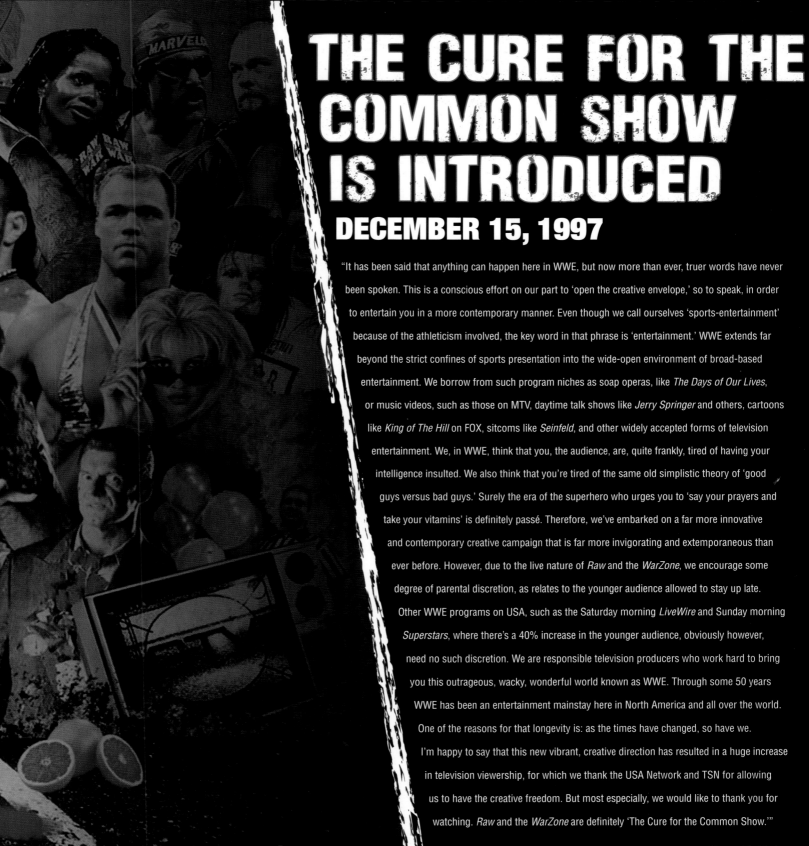

THE CURE FOR THE COMMON SHOW IS INTRODUCED

DECEMBER 15, 1997

"It has been said that anything can happen here in WWE, but now more than ever, truer words have never been spoken. This is a conscious effort on our part to 'open the creative envelope,' so to speak, in order to entertain you in a more contemporary manner. Even though we call ourselves 'sports-entertainment' because of the athleticism involved, the key word in that phrase is 'entertainment.' WWE extends far beyond the strict confines of sports presentation into the wide-open environment of broad-based entertainment. We borrow from such program niches as soap operas, like *The Days of Our Lives*, or music videos, such as those on MTV, daytime talk shows like *Jerry Springer* and others, cartoons like *King of The Hill* on FOX, sitcoms like *Seinfeld*, and other widely accepted forms of television entertainment. We, in WWE, think that you, the audience, are, quite frankly, tired of having your intelligence insulted. We also think that you're tired of the same old simplistic theory of 'good guys versus bad guys.' Surely the era of the superhero who urges you to 'say your prayers and take your vitamins' is definitely passé. Therefore, we've embarked on a far more innovative and contemporary creative campaign that is far more invigorating and extemporaneous than ever before. However, due to the live nature of *Raw* and the *WarZone*, we encourage some degree of parental discretion, as relates to the younger audience allowed to stay up late. Other WWE programs on USA, such as the Saturday morning *LiveWire* and Sunday morning *Superstars*, where there's a 40% increase in the younger audience, obviously however, need no such discretion. We are responsible television producers who work hard to bring you this outrageous, wacky, wonderful world known as WWE. Through some 50 years WWE has been an entertainment mainstay here in North America and all over the world. One of the reasons for that longevity is: as the times have changed, so have we. I'm happy to say that this new vibrant, creative direction has resulted in a huge increase in television viewership, for which we thank the USA Network and TSN for allowing us to have the creative freedom. But most especially, we would like to thank you for watching. *Raw* and the *WarZone* are definitely 'The Cure for the Common Show.'"

—Vince McMahon

CONTENTS

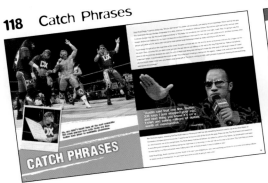
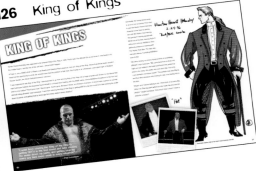

"WWE had to change what they were doing as the characters and storylines they had developed were getting stale. They had a guy in Stone Cold Steve Austin who had that attitude in real life, and it translated to the TV screen."

—Jim Ross

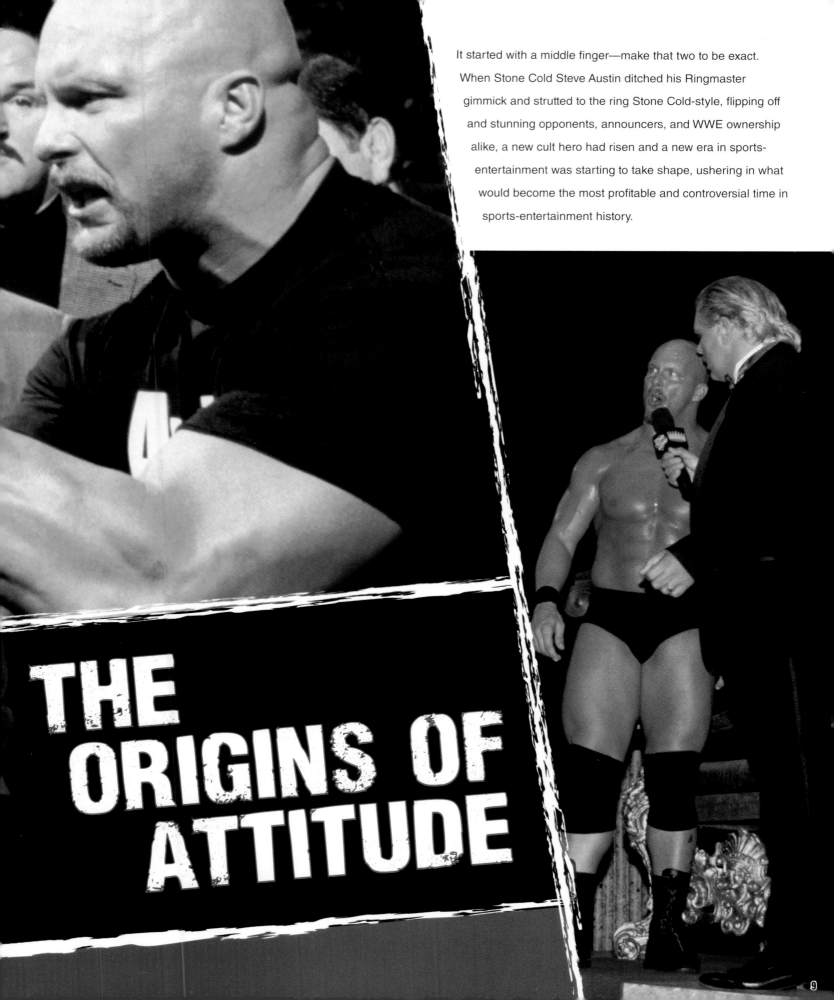

It started with a middle finger—make that two to be exact. When Stone Cold Steve Austin ditched his Ringmaster gimmick and strutted to the ring Stone Cold-style, flipping off and stunning opponents, announcers, and WWE ownership alike, a new cult hero had risen and a new era in sports-entertainment was starting to take shape, ushering in what would become the most profitable and controversial time in sports-entertainment history.

THE ORIGINS OF ATTITUDE

"I think when you look back at that time period, you can't just pick out one instance and say, there it is, that's when the Attitude Era began," reflects Hall of Famer Jim Ross, who served as both announcer and Head of Talent Relations during the time period. "But it was time for a change in the industry. WWE had to change what they were doing as the characters and storylines they had developed were getting stale. They had a guy in Stone Cold Steve Austin who had that attitude in real life, and it translated to the TV screen."

When Stone Cold Steve Austin cut his now infamous (and unscripted) promo at *King of the Ring* 1996, everyone knew the business was about to transform. Austin told Jake "The Snake" Roberts, "You sit there and you thump your bible and you say your prayers, and it didn't get you anywhere. Talk about your Psalms, talk about John 3:16; Austin 3:16 says I just whipped your ass." From the locker room to the arena seats, it was clear that Austin 3:16 would be leading the new breed of Attitude.

"The Attitude Era was about characters that people loved, and no matter who you were, there was a character for you to root for or against."

—Ron Simmons

"We went to *Raw* the next night, and Austin 3:16 signs were everywhere," remembers Ross. "It was just what the business needed."

The increased competition from rivals WCW and ECW, as WCW management opened their wallets to steal superstars like Lex Luger and WWE women's champ Alundra Blayze (who threw her WWE Women's Title in the trash on live TV), sparked what would become the Monday Night War between WCW *Nitro* and *Raw*. Meanwhile, upstart and ultra-violent ECW, led by owner Paul Heyman, looked to steal the spotlight by increasing the danger of stunts, while introducing more risqué storylines into the world of sports-entertainment.

"This was a time when WWE was facing some very serious threats to its own livelihood," says Ross.

"At this point, it was time to adapt or there was real concern of extinction. The uniqueness of the time is that we had the edge of competing against Turner. This made our situation unique because it was the first time in my career that two national companies were going head-to-head at the same time on competing cable networks. A lot of people also overlook the fact that TNT was the number one rated cable network in America, so it wasn't like when TNA tried to go head-to-head against WWE with Spike. That would be like an Arena League team trying to compete against *Sunday Night Football*, it's just not going to work. Back when WWE was competing with WCW, it was two giants going head-to-head, and WCW made a big splash when they went out and started signing talent like Kevin Nash and Scott Hall. WWE needed a new direction."

"I was really angry and felt threatened by Ted Turner and his organization because they owned networks," says Vince McMahon. "It's one thing to be in competition with us; fine that's the great American way. It's another to come right at me and to try to diminish my audience, which in my view was Ted's plan. Ted's plan was to hurt his opponent. So if he could hurt us, then he could outlast us. This is my philosophy. I have never heard Ted say this; this is what I think to be the truth. So why else, if you own networks and you can put a television show on whenever you wish, why would you do it directly against us? The only logical reason is to hurt us. Then furthering that, he would play a few tricks. He would come on the air earlier. He would stay later. He did all sorts of tricks that I didn't particularly appreciate."

Then again, Vince McMahon had something Turner couldn't replicate (or buy): The swagger and the attitude that was Stone Cold.

"When you made a mistake in the locker room in the Attitude Era, they ate your ass alive and rolled along with 'We're happy you couldn't keep up.'"

—Big Show

WWE experimented with more adult-themed storylines. Brian Pillman's Loose Cannon character even helped push Steve Austin to the point of invading Pillman's house. Pillman retaliated by pulling a gun in a scene more reminiscent of an R-rated action flick than anything ever performed during a small-screen sports-entertainment program.

Add that to the increasing outrageous crotch-chopping antics of D-Generation X, a group defined by pushing the censors' limits with their double entendres and "suck it" bravado, and WWE had found a new recipe for success.

"Really, for me, it was when Shawn and Hunter just started doing whatever they wanted—that's when the Attitude Era began," says Road Dogg. "People were like, holy mackerel, what are they doing with that sausage? I felt D-Generation X was the catalyst for the era because they reached out to the degenerates. People tuned in to see what DX was going to do next, and then they saw guys like Austin and Pillman and were glued to the show."

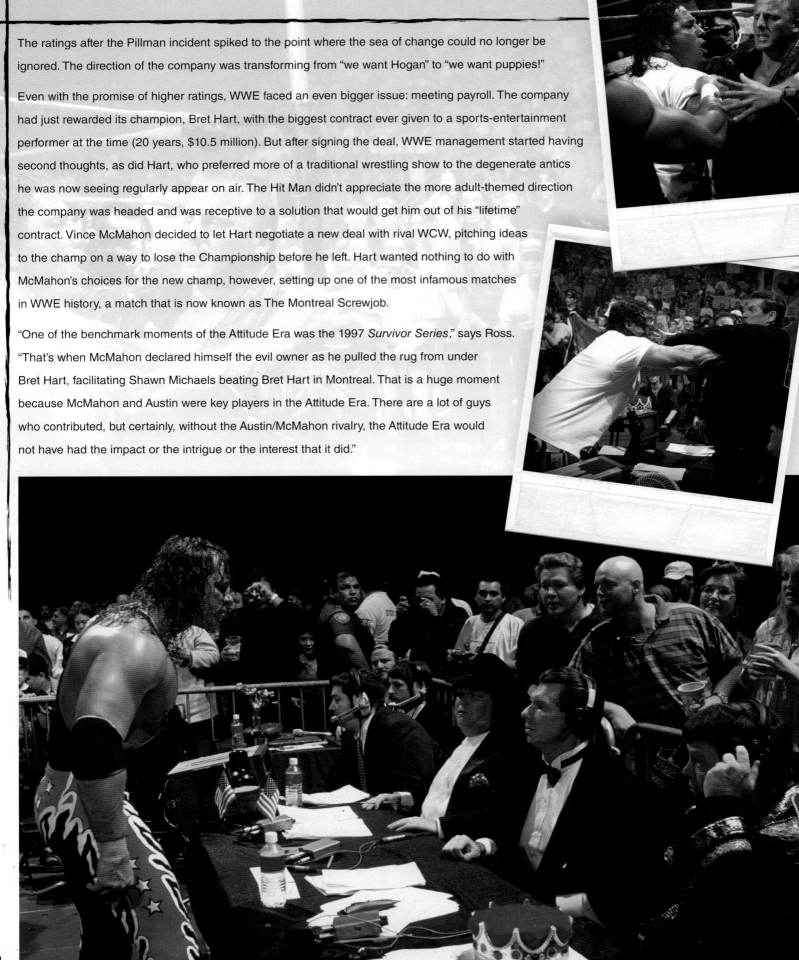

The ratings after the Pillman incident spiked to the point where the sea of change could no longer be ignored. The direction of the company was transforming from "we want Hogan" to "we want puppies!"

Even with the promise of higher ratings, WWE faced an even bigger issue: meeting payroll. The company had just rewarded its champion, Bret Hart, with the biggest contract ever given to a sports-entertainment performer at the time (20 years, $10.5 million). But after signing the deal, WWE management started having second thoughts, as did Hart, who preferred more of a traditional wrestling show to the degenerate antics he was now seeing regularly appear on air. The Hit Man didn't appreciate the more adult-themed direction the company was headed and was receptive to a solution that would get him out of his "lifetime" contract. Vince McMahon decided to let Hart negotiate a new deal with rival WCW, pitching ideas to the champ on a way to lose the Championship before he left. Hart wanted nothing to do with McMahon's choices for the new champ, however, setting up one of the most infamous matches in WWE history, a match that is now known as The Montreal Screwjob.

"One of the benchmark moments of the Attitude Era was the 1997 *Survivor Series*," says Ross. "That's when McMahon declared himself the evil owner as he pulled the rug from under Bret Hart, facilitating Shawn Michaels beating Bret Hart in Montreal. That is a huge moment because McMahon and Austin were key players in the Attitude Era. There are a lot of guys who contributed, but certainly, without the Austin/McMahon rivalry, the Attitude Era would not have had the impact or the intrigue or the interest that it did."

A few months after Montreal, Vince McMahon made the era official, opening the December 15, 1997 *Raw* by telling viewers that the WWE now required parental discretion for younger viewers. This was a first for WWE, not only in the fact that they were about to up the level of violence, foul language, and Diva skin, but for the fact that Vince McMahon was speaking directly to the audience as the WWE owner. *Raw* was now "the cure for the common show" and it was unlike anything ever seen in sports entertainment.

In a matter of weeks, *Raw*'s ratings jumped. The WWE audience tuned in to see everything from Val Venis' porn star gimmick, complete with Money Shot finishing move, to a pimp with a "Ho Train" to a Superstar who was known for vomiting on command.

"We had to change some things," says Ross. "We had to bring in new talent. And that talent brought an attitude, a hunger, an aggressiveness that the old roster was lacking. The decision creatively was made to switch from a more traditional—kind of like it is today with the PG rating—to a PG-14 scenario. Changing the scenario was like changing from having a typical radio show to having a radio show on Sirius XM. You are free to do a lot more things on satellite radio than you are on terrestrial radio. TV-14 opened up the envelope and allowed creative to do more risqué things. Some of them were very, very successful, and some of them were hideous. But in any event, more often than not, it got people talking around the water cooler on Tuesday morning, and that was one of the goals. We needed to get people talking about our product again."

While the new talent began to shine, it was the fight between Vince McMahon and Austin's anti-hero that took center stage. The crowd surged behind the fight of the common man against authority.

All the while, new Superstars and storylines were being introduced on the undercard with characters like fun-loving baby-faced Rocky Maivia recast as trash-talking villain, The Rock.

"When you look back at the Attitude Era, everyone remembers the crazy moments they still show replays of today," says Hall of Famer Ron Simmons. "But to me, what made the time period special was the level of depth we had on the card. The Attitude Era was about characters that people loved, and no matter who you were, there was a character for you to root for or against. Everybody on the card did something and contributed in ways that people could relate to. Black people, clowns, funny people, bad asses, athletes—it didn't matter what you wanted to see; we had it. I think it's a bit too one-dimensional now. Everybody wants to look like a cloned body builder, but that's not what people want. That's not what people see in their everyday lives. That's why the Attitude Era was so memorable to so many people, because the era offered something for everybody to get something out of."

"Our roster dictated the direction of our company," says Ross. "They had a look and feel that was very much one made up of attitude. We had comprised the roster of many competitive people, guys who had come from a mainstream sports background. So not only were they competitive about getting that top spot and making the most money in our locker room, but they were also competitive in looking at the competition from WCW. Every Tuesday, the scorecard would reflect who won the television ratings."

Unfortunately for WWE, that scorecard was still extremely one-sided, with *Nitro* winning the ratings war for nearly two years, a score that irked the WWE locker room and drove the competitive athletes to push the envelope even further.

"They beat us 83 weeks in a row," says Ross. "If you're a football team or a basketball team or any other sports team and you lose 83 weeks in a row, the management and the coaching staff probably would've been gone. The difference in our situation was that our leader was the owner of the company. We knew that we had to steer the course. There was never a week that went by that I didn't think we'd eventually win the competition. I was a competitive person, and I just knew that if we kept doing the right things, if we could recruit new talent, recruit the most talented, charismatic athletes, then I knew we'd be OK in the long run."

"When you look back at the roster we were assembling at the time," continues Ross, "we had depth, and I took pride in that. I looked at it like I was a recruiter at a D-1 school. The more competition and the more good players you have, the better your team is going to be. We were not one-dimensional."

A strong leader also made all of the difference. "McMahon had no issues letting it be known who the boss of the company was, which really played into WWE's favor," says Ross. "Not only was it important on screen and in character, but also behind the scenes. Compare it to WCW, where they had too many cooks in the kitchen. We had one chef, and whether he was right or wrong, we got our marching orders from Vince. He loved being Mr. McMahon. It wasn't a stretch from his true personality. He was the alpha male, and he had to be the alpha male. You're not managing a locker room full of choir boys. These guys need leadership. Athletes want structure. Athletes want leadership. Having Vince be that one leader, where you could go to one guy and get a straight answer is huge. You might not always like the straight answer, but at least you got one, and that wasn't always the case in WCW."

"Vince McMahon became a billionaire based on the Attitude Era, and Attitude was spawned by the ECW experience."

—Paul Heyman

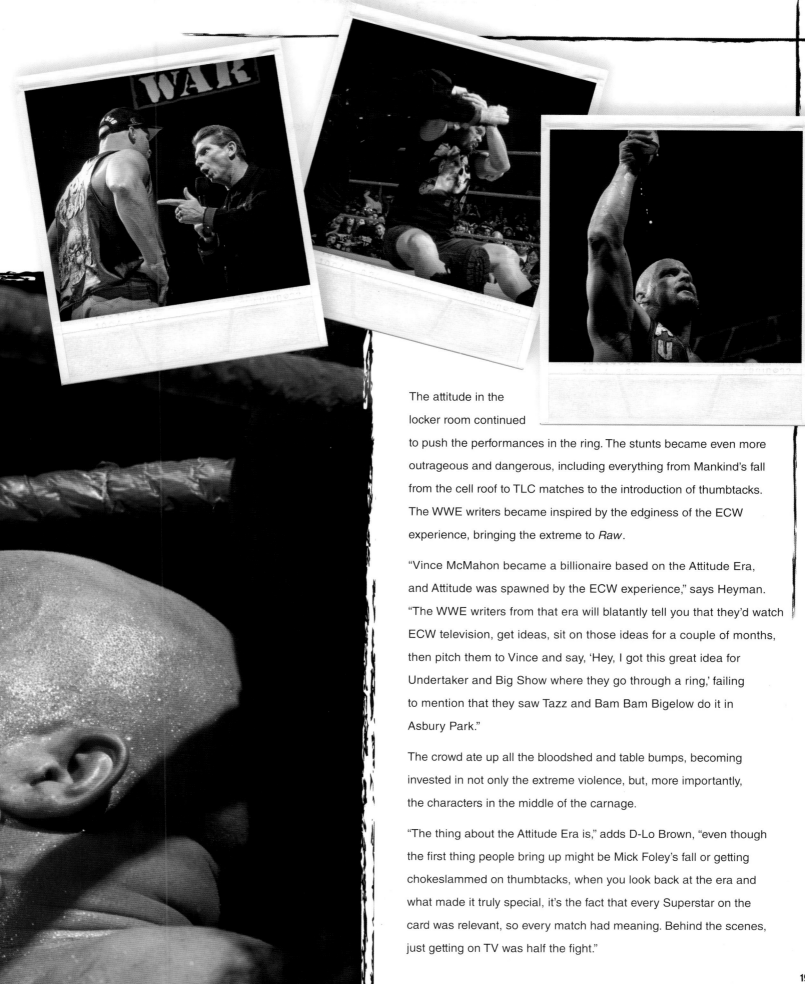

The attitude in the locker room continued to push the performances in the ring. The stunts became even more outrageous and dangerous, including everything from Mankind's fall from the cell roof to TLC matches to the introduction of thumbtacks. The WWE writers became inspired by the edginess of the ECW experience, bringing the extreme to *Raw*.

"Vince McMahon became a billionaire based on the Attitude Era, and Attitude was spawned by the ECW experience," says Heyman. "The WWE writers from that era will blatantly tell you that they'd watch ECW television, get ideas, sit on those ideas for a couple of months, then pitch them to Vince and say, 'Hey, I got this great idea for Undertaker and Big Show where they go through a ring,' failing to mention that they saw Tazz and Bam Bam Bigelow do it in Asbury Park."

The crowd ate up all the bloodshed and table bumps, becoming invested in not only the extreme violence, but, more importantly, the characters in the middle of the carnage.

"The thing about the Attitude Era is," adds D-Lo Brown, "even though the first thing people bring up might be Mick Foley's fall or getting chokeslammed on thumbtacks, when you look back at the era and what made it truly special, it's the fact that every Superstar on the card was relevant, so every match had meaning. Behind the scenes, just getting on TV was half the fight."

"The roster we were building intimidated people. There were no boys; we were all men," says Mark Henry. "And we would all do anything to outdo each other. That's what was happening on a nightly basis. Somebody would say, 'Hey, I'm going to jump off the top of a cage,' and somebody else would say, 'Well, I'm going to pick somebody up over my head and throw them to the floor.' Stuff started happening that you never saw before, and it was because we were trying to beat not only WCW, but we were also trying to outdo everyone else in the locker room."

"People don't realize it, but there was a lot of 'I will cut your throat to get my segment on TV,'" says Big Show. "It wasn't buddy-buddy, 'Hey, let me show you how to do this, and maybe you should work on that.' When you made a mistake in the locker room in the Attitude Era, they ate your ass alive and rolled along with 'We're happy you couldn't keep up.'"

To Ross, this type of competitiveness just added fuel to the fire. "We had a lot of guys who we hired and we brought in who wanted to be main event players, and that was good. Some people may have been concerned that you might have civil unrest in your locker room, but that never bothered me. That's a matter of communicating with talent and how you coach them and how you lead them. I was never too intimidated by the potential of civil unrest. I wanted every guy to try to steal the show from everybody else, and that's what ended up happening."

"Before you knew it, people started changing that channel," says Ross. They wanted to see what our young stars were doing. Once the Attitude Era found its stride, it wouldn't be much longer before WCW started to crumble and *Raw* was back to being number one. With the talent we assembled and the storylines playing out on the card from top to bottom, it was inevitable WWE would be back on top. Our talent had the attitude we needed to win."

> "The roster we were building intimidated people. There were no boys; we were all men."
>
> —Mark Henry

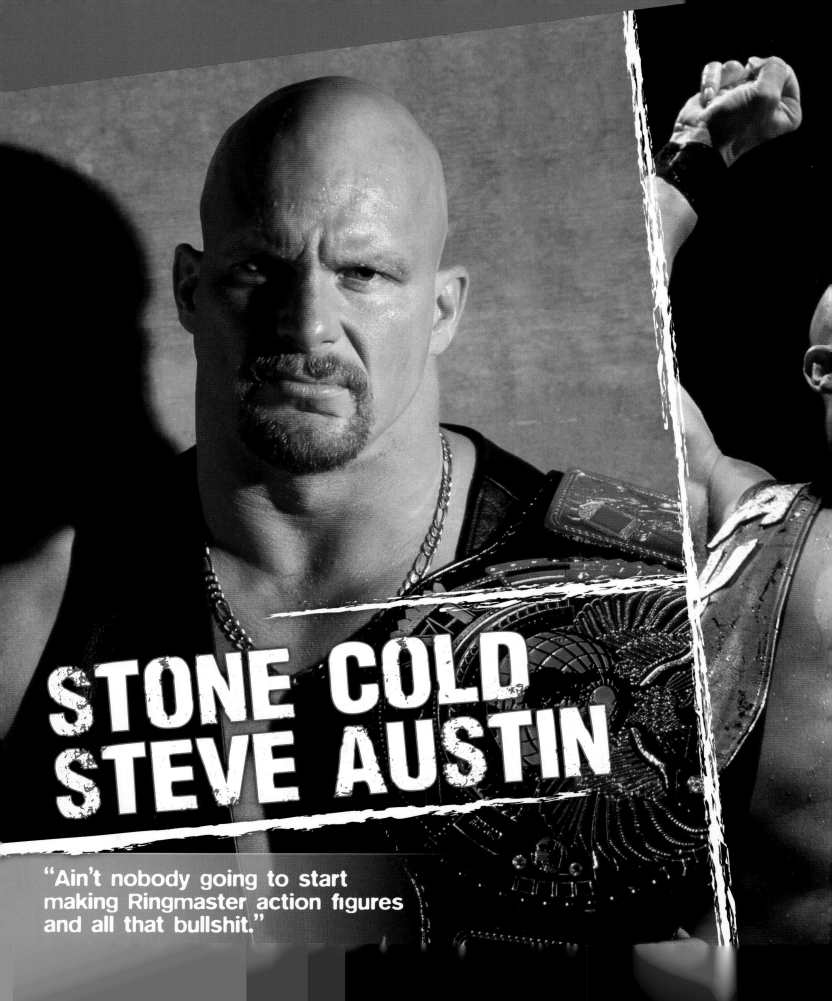

STONE COLD STEVE AUSTIN

"Ain't nobody going to start making Ringmaster action figures and all that bullshit."

"No one wanted to see 'Ringmaster' on a t-shirt." Those are the words of Stone Cold Steve Austin, talking about making the switch from a gimmick going nowhere to catching fire as Stone Cold.

"Ain't nobody going to start making Ringmaster action figures and all that bullshit," says Austin, who broke out of his Ringmaster rut and helped spark the Attitude Era with a trademark nasty streak, middle-finger salute, and Austin 3:16 t-shirts.

As Austin's popularity grew, backstage, Vince McMahon and the creative team could feel the groundswell. Says Austin: "I was starting to get some momentum as Stone Cold Steve Austin. I had a talk with Vince; he was going to stop editing my lines. He let me be me. He let me talk this south Texas horse shit I grew up hearing. My attitude and everything was totally honed in, I was dialed in, and I was a walking, talking whoop-ass machine."

Austin's whoop-ass machine not only went on to adlib some of the most famous lines of the Attitude Era—"because Stone Cold said so"—but also championed the cause of the everyman, taking the fight to his boss and The Corporation in one of WWE history's most memorable rivalries.

But it almost didn't happen, thanks to a terrifying moment at *SummerSlam* 1997 that forced Austin out of action for several months. The timing for The Rattlesnake could not have been worse, as his white-hot momentum was only just beginning to simmer. Austin was able to muster enough strength to roll up Owen Hart for the win, but the proud Superstar was left with serious questions about his future in the ring.

Stone Cold recalls the conclusion to the match: "Owen starts walking around the ring, teasing the crowd. There was a stipulation in this match; if I didn't win, I had to kiss his ass. So he's walking around, saying, 'Now he's going to kiss my ass! I'm thinking, 'I got to find a way to get out of this match. I got to find a way to take care of that stipulation so I don't have to kiss someone's ass.'

Austin was able to spare himself this indignity. Still, several question marks lingered. Heading into SummerSlam, Austin was standing right at the cusp of superstardom, perhaps greater than the type Hulk Hogan enjoyed during the mid 1980s. Now as he contemplated his future, it was unclear if he would ever be able to recapture the same mojo. Doubting Stone Cold, however, is usually an exercise in futility.

When Stone Cold finally returned to *Raw*, the Rattlesnake was hungry for revenge, setting his sights not only on Hart but on the new Intercontinental Champion, The Rock. Austin defeated The Rock to win back his vacated Intercontinental title. But when Mr. McMahon ordered a rematch, Austin instead tossed the championship, along with The Rock's pager and cell phone, off a bridge and into the New Hampshire river, telling the crowd: "Let him swim out there and find the damn thing. If he gets lucky, maybe he'll find it. If he don't, maybe he'll drown. I really don't give a damn what he does."

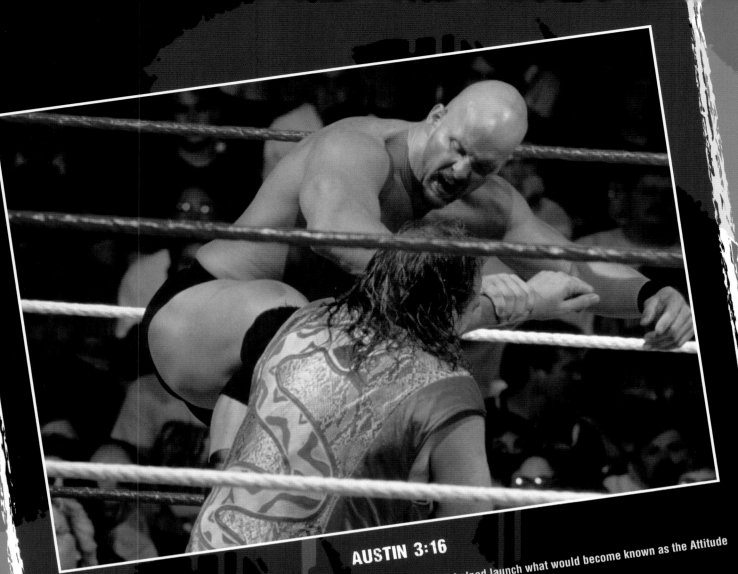

AUSTIN 3:16

Stone Cold Steve Austin's uncensored and edgy promo at *King of the Ring* 1996 helped launch what would become known as the Attitude Era. Austin breaks down the promo's origins:

"We go to *King of the Ring* and I'm wrestling Marc Mero in the first match, a tournament style pay-per-view. We're doing a little move that he does, and he kicks me in my damn mouth and busts my lip wide open. I wrestle the rest of the match with a busted lip, all screwed up inside there. I beat Marc Mero, and I'm going to the back, bleeding outta my mouth. I needed 14 stitches to close up my lip. So I go to the hospital in an ambulance, in my work gear, and come back with 14 stitches in my mouth. And I know I'm going to wrestle Jake 'The Snake' Roberts in the final. Now, at the time, Jake, who's one of the greatest talkers of all time, one of my favorite workers of all time, was kind of going through a little religious moment in his life. He would go around and do religious testimony to people and talk about evil and drugs and everything else. So, in the time I was gone, he had cut a religious-based promo.

"Well, as soon as I got out of that ambulance, Jake had cut the promo. I got out of the ambulance, and there was Michael PS Hayes, one of my favorite wrestlers of all time that I used to watch in Dallas, Texas. He's going to be the guy interviewing me after I win *KOTR*. He goes, 'Steve, I just want you to know that, while you were gone, Jake cut a religious-based promo on you.' 'Alright, thanks Michael.' Bam, it hit me, just like that. I thought about, okay, religious—Austin 3:16 popped into my head. Back in the day, if you went to a football game or watched it on TV, when they went to kick the extra point or a field goal, there would always be a giant John 3:16 sign in the end zone crowd. So I said, okay, Austin 3:16. I thought about it as soon as he told me, that instant. And I said, I got something for his ass. I totally went out there—we had basically a short match, because my lip was busted with those 14 stitches— but I went out there, had a short match, beat Jake, and there it was, off to go talk to Michael PS Hayes on that *KOTR* acceptance speech. And he asked me a question, and I spit out that program and I was running down Jake. I still remember bits and pieces like it was yesterday. This was all adlibbed; this wasn't anything someone handed to me on a piece of paper. It was what I was feeling. It was from my heart and my guts and what was going on inside my brain … nothing but attitude."

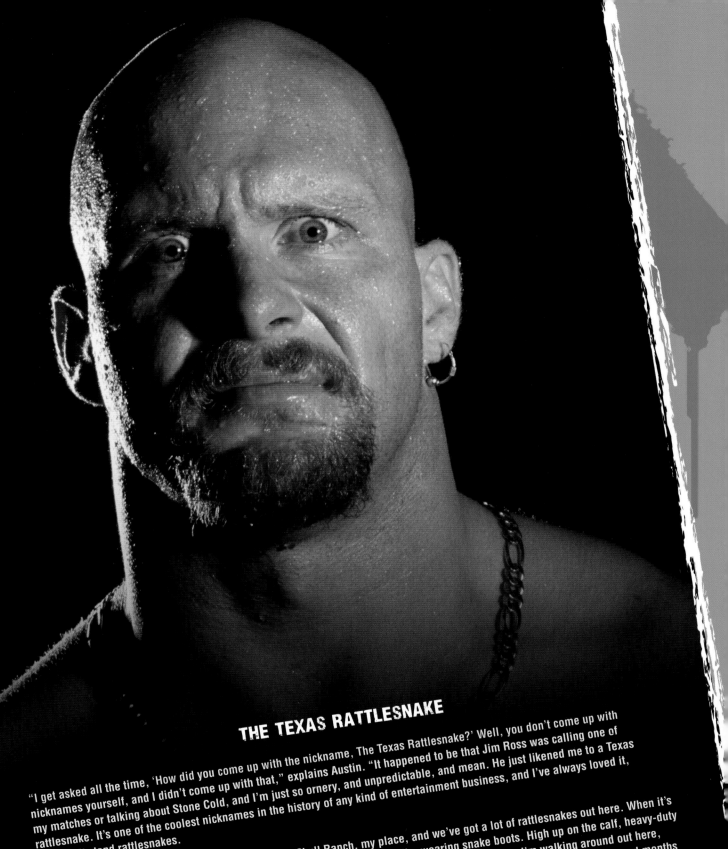

THE TEXAS RATTLESNAKE

"I get asked all the time, 'How did you come up with the nickname, The Texas Rattlesnake?' Well, you don't come up with nicknames yourself, and I didn't come up with that," explains Austin. "It happened to be that Jim Ross was calling one of my matches or talking about Stone Cold, and I'm just so ornery, and unpredictable, and mean. He just likened me to a Texas rattlesnake. It's one of the coolest nicknames in the history of any kind of entertainment business, and I've always loved it, but I can't stand rattlesnakes.

"We're out here in South Texas, we're at the Broken Skull Ranch, my place, and we've got a lot of rattlesnakes out here. When it's as hot as it is right here, right now, normally anytime I'm doing anything, I'm wearing snake boots. High up on the calf, heavy-duty material to keep from snake bites. I don't like snakes. There's a bunch of them out here. Any time I'm walking around out here, I'm watching where I'm walking, because you don't want to step on one of those bastards. If they bite you, it's months and months of rehabilitation and rotted, dead tissue. It's a bad day at the office if you get bit by a Texas Rattlesnake—this one, too."

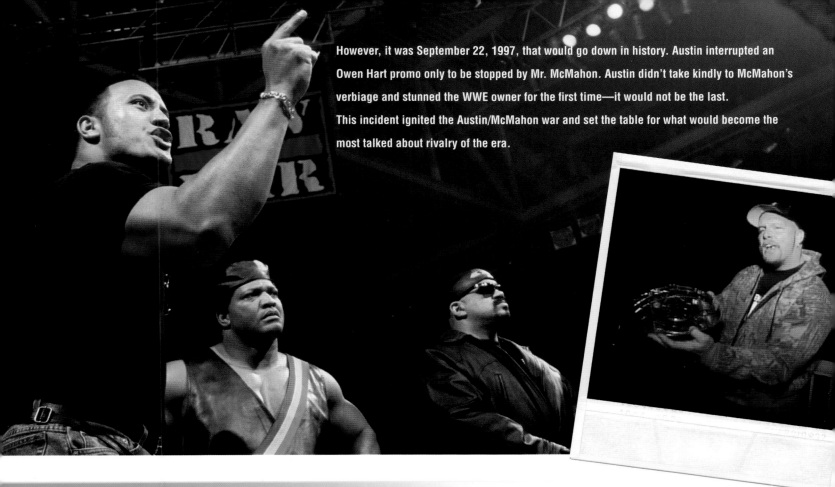

However, it was September 22, 1997, that would go down in history. Austin interrupted an Owen Hart promo only to be stopped by Mr. McMahon. Austin didn't take kindly to McMahon's verbiage and stunned the WWE owner for the first time—it would not be the last. This incident ignited the Austin/McMahon war and set the table for what would become the most talked about rivalry of the era.

"I'll tell you what, once you stun Vince McMahon you're in for the long haul."
— Stone Cold Steve Austin

Says Austin: "I had that altercation in the middle of the ring with Vince. Out of the blue, I hit that son of a bitch with a Stone Cold Stunner, and the roof came off that Madison Square Garden. The roof probably came off of every single house that was watching *Monday Night Raw* that night. It blew the roof off of every damn thing that was watching or had a TV in that room … it was something magical. And I'll say this about Vince: I love working with Vince McMahon in a match or an angle, but he's not the most graceful human being in the world. When I kicked him in the gut to set up that Stunner, he bent down a little too far; I had to make sure I had him by his damn neck before I could drop him in that Stone Cold Stunner, and you know we could have botched it. Now, had we botched the first Stone Cold Stunner on Vince McMahon, it would have been the drizzling shits. We pulled it off and he took it, and when he did that quivering thing with his eyes open like a crappie on a bass boat, it was the greatest thing in the world. People ate that shit up, and I'll tell you what, once you stun Vince McMahon you're in for the long haul."

When Mr. McMahon brought the iconic but volatile boxer "Iron" Mike Tyson to Raw, Stone Cold saw the perfect opportunity not only to ruin the owner's big score, but to grab headlines around the world by flipping off Tyson and spurring one of Raw's wildest brawls.

"I mean, man, things were hauling ass, white hot, and then Vince gets this idea to bring Mike Tyson into the picture. He starts talking about what we're going to do and how we're going to bring him into Monday Night Raw, and I was going to interrupt this segment and get into an altercation with Mike Tyson. And I said god dang, that's badass. That's going to be some good shit," says Austin. "You know, it was the damnedest thing. Mike Tyson's in the middle of the ring and, crash, here comes Stone Cold's music. And I'll tell you what, that crowd went ape shit. When you have Mike Tyson and Vince McMahon in the ring, and here comes old Stone Cold, that's hotter than fire, and there are going to be some eyes glued to the TV set. I got out to the ring and I did my drive-by on him, did all my turnbuckles, and basically started cutting a promo on him, the promo that you've seen a million times.

"Then I put the double birds in Mike Tyson's face and, boy, he didn't think too much of that. He shoves me across the ring. I'll tell you something: when I went back at Mike Tyson, I was trying to get that son of a bitch. You watch those producers hold me down, that shit was a shoot—I was going for Mike Tyson's ass. Now, I knew he was going to punch me, but I was going after him. You fucking push me across the ring, we're going to do this deal. I'm going to make this shit real, because everything in that ring is real.

"Man, I'll tell you what, when he [Vince McMahon] brought Mike Tyson to the mix, a mainstream guy who's one of the greatest boxers of all time, this tough guy that was this walking disaster, the baddest man on two feet, it brought so many outside eyeballs to our product, and it crossed us over.

"Then I put the double birds in Mike Tyson's face and, boy, he didn't think too much of that. He shoves me across the ring. I'll tell you something; when I went back at Mike Tyson, I was trying to get that son of a bitch."

—Stone Cold Steve Austin

"I mean, everybody was talking about that, and Vince hit a grand slam with that idea. We were on SportsCenter, we were on every news show across the world, and that was instrumental and huge for us to separate ourselves from WCW in the Monday Night War. It was just like when they send one of those rockets into space; you always have that pack and it goes off, and the rocket keeps going higher. We used Mike Tyson as another rocket pack, and the ship kept going higher and things got hotter and hotter. But it was very important in what happened with my career and in the business, because once you do business with Mike Tyson, you know that the world is watching."

"I ran off the top of that thing and hit Vince with the Flying Clothesline, and the place just blew up," laughs Austin. "That was a blast."

— Stone Cold Steve Austin

The Stone Cold madness had turned into a pop culture phenomenon, with the iconic black Austin 3:16 shirts selling out around the world. Austin won the WWE Championship at WrestleMania XIV alongside special referee Mike Tyson. After capturing the title, Austin continued his quest to fight the fight for the everyman, spitting in the face of authority while becoming even more of a sore spot for Mr. McMahon. Austin humiliated the WWE owner by filling his Corvette with cement, smacking him with a bedpan, and even soaking his corporation with a beer bath.

Austin's favorite moment? Crashing the Zamboni into the ring in Detroit. "I ran off the top of that thing and hit Vince with the Flying Clothesline, and the place just blew up," laughs Austin. "That was a blast."

"To some degree, Steve had a chip on his shoulder when he got to WWE because of how his journey had transpired since he had gotten into the business. He had a number of false starts where it looked like he was going to do this or that, but somebody in power abruptly changed their minds. So, by the time he got to us, he had this angry, anti-establishment attitude, and for good reason. He didn't like the establishment, he didn't trust us. But, boy, did he have that animalistic magnitude the fans are attracted to. I remember one night after a TV taping, I went back to the locker room and I said, 'Hey Steve, good job tonight. You know, sooner than later, you're going to be a big babyface.' And he just started cussing like I just told him his hunting dog got run over by a cement truck or a hot coal flipped into his ass. He hated the thought of being a babyface. What he was thinking, though, was more of a traditional babyface, just like we tried to present with The Rock. He said, 'I didn't come here to be a babyface!' and he went on this tirade, cussing in general, because he was off on this track of being this badass, and he didn't want a creative hiccup to knock him off track again.

"He didn't have faith in the estab... establishment failed him time and time again through... years. Next time I saw him, I had accounting do some research on what some guys had made on their quarterly royalty checks. A lot of the babyfaces had received some massive royalty checks over the years for selling t-shirts, foam fingers, and caps. Most of the guys who made the money back then on the royalties were the fan favorites. I said, 'Steve, look, this guy just got a six-figure-plus royalty check just for a quarter of a year's sales.' It was at that point that he realized that being a fan favorite might not be too bad of an idea after all, especially if he didn't have to change his overall persona. He could be a badass babyface, and that fit perfectly into the Attitude Era because he showed natural disgust and disdain against the establishment, and he had an amazing chemistry with McMahon that we could've never created out of thin air. Austin and McMahon were the two primary entities who defined the Attitude Era, without question."

I've had a lot of rivalries in my career. Some real important rivalries with some great people who I love to be in the ring with. But my rivalry with Stone Cold vs. Mr. McMahon … it was the best of all time. It really was the most important one that I was in. It took our action, our level, higher and brought in even more eyeballs, and just made people want to tune into Monday Night Raw to see what the hell these guys were going to do to each other next. And, to me, it was just a basic, regular, everyday guy, Stone Cold Steve Austin, who was pissed off at the system. And the system was always trying to hold him down. And Vince McMahon was the owner of the company, the guy pulling all the strings and running everything. He was trying to get me to be a corporate guy, and you're never going to get Stone Cold Steve Austin to be that guy.

"I think one of the reasons that the Stone Cold/Mr. McMahon rivalry resonated so well with the fans was that, at some point, every man or woman wants to punch their boss in the mouth for making them do this, that, or whatever, and it's just the way it is. And Stone Cold Steve Austin got to give his boss hell each and every single week. The thing about myself and Vince, we just had a great chemistry. It's just hard to describe and put into words, but anytime I stepped in the ring with him, anytime I got in front of the camera with him, anytime we were going to do a promo, it didn't matter. I was feeding off of him and he was feeding off of me, and that's just the way it was."

"My attitude and everything was totally honed in, I was dialed in, and I was a walking, talking whoop-ass machine."

— Stone Cold Steve Austin

20 MATCHES THAT DEFINED THE ERA

STONE COLD STEVE AUSTIN vs. THE ROCK

MATCH TYPE	No Disqualification
EVENT	*WrestleMania X-Seven*
DATE	April 1, 2001
VENUE	The Reliant Astrodome
LOCATION	Houston, Texas

RESULT: Stone Cold gets an assist from Vince McMahon, turning heel and shocking the WWE Universe in the process, to win the WWE Championship.

TRIPLE H vs. STONE COLD STEVE AUSTIN

MATCH TYPE	3 Stages of Hell
EVENT	*No Way Out*
DATE	February 25, 2001
VENUE	Thomas and Mack Center
LOCATION	Las Vegas, Nevada

RESULT: Triple H drops the first fall, only to come back and defeat Austin 2-1 by winning both the Street Fight and Steel Cage Match.

THE ROCK vs. MANKIND

MATCH TYPE	I Quit Match
EVENT	*Royal Rumble*
DATE	January 24, 1999
VENUE	Arrowhead Pond
LOCATION	Anaheim, California

RESULT: The Rock brutalizes Mankind in and out of the ring until Mankind is heard shouting "I quit!" three times in a row, handing the victory to The Rock. Later, it is revealed that the audio was from one of Mankind's promos leading up to the match, giving The Rock a devious win.

UNDERTAKER vs. STONE COLD STEVE AUSTIN

MATCH TYPE	First Blood
EVENT	*Fully Loaded*
DATE	July 25, 1999
VENUE	Marine Midland Arena
LOCATION	Buffalo, New York

RESULT: This match stipulates that if Stone Cold wins, Vince McMahon could never appear on WWE television again. With that prize at stake, Stone Cold Steve Austin hits Undertaker with a television camera to get the blood flowing and win the match.

EDGE and CHRISTIAN vs. THE HARDY BOYZ vs. THE DUDLEY BOYZ

MATCH TYPE	TLC II
EVENT	*WrestleMania X-Seven*
DATE	April 1, 2001
VENUE	The Reliant Astrodome
LOCATION	Houston, Texas

RESULT: After Edge delivers a flying spear off the ladder, onto a dangling Jeff Hardy, Christian receives a boost up to the titles from Rhyno to capture tag team gold.

TRIPLE H vs. CACTUS JACK

MATCH TYPE	Street Fight
EVENT	*Royal Rumble*
DATE	January 23, 2000
VENUE	Madison Square Garden
LOCATION	New York, New York

RESULT: Triple H performs a Pedigree, sending Cactus Jack face-first into a pile of thumbtacks for the win.

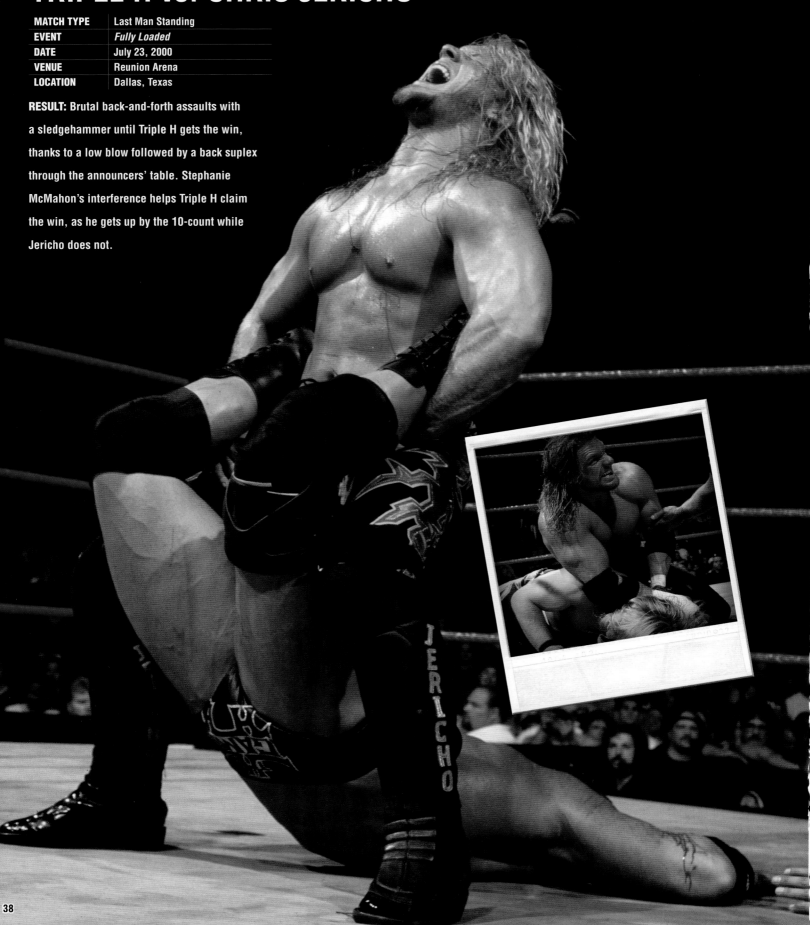

TRIPLE H vs. CHRIS JERICHO

MATCH TYPE	Last Man Standing
EVENT	*Fully Loaded*
DATE	July 23, 2000
VENUE	Reunion Arena
LOCATION	Dallas, Texas

RESULT: Brutal back-and-forth assaults with a sledgehammer until Triple H gets the win, thanks to a low blow followed by a back suplex through the announcers' table. Stephanie McMahon's interference helps Triple H claim the win, as he gets up by the 10-count while Jericho does not.

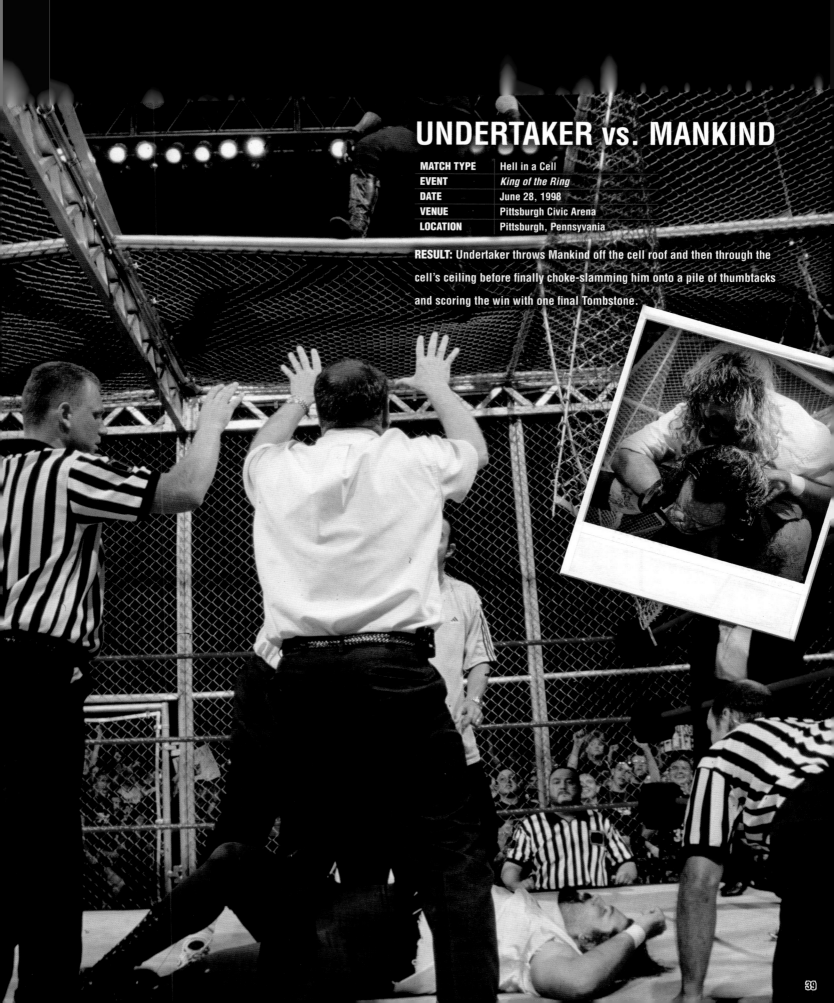

UNDERTAKER vs. MANKIND

MATCH TYPE	Hell in a Cell
EVENT	*King of the Ring*
DATE	June 28, 1998
VENUE	Pittsburgh Civic Arena
LOCATION	Pittsburgh, Pennsyvania

RESULT: Undertaker throws Mankind off the cell roof and then through the cell's ceiling before finally choke-slamming him onto a pile of thumbtacks and scoring the win with one final Tombstone.

CHRIS JERICHO vs. CHRIS BENOIT

MATCH TYPE	Ladder Match
EVENT	*Royal Rumble*
DATE	January 21, 2001
VENUE	New Orleans Arena
LOCATION	New Orleans, Louisiana

RESULT: Chris Jericho knocks Benoit over the top rope before ascending the ladder to capture the Intercontinental Championship.

KURT ANGLE vs. STONE COLD STEVE AUSTIN vs. TRIPLE H vs. THE ROCK vs. UNDERTAKER vs. RIKISHI

MATCH TYPE	Hell in a Cell
EVENT	*Armageddon*
DATE	December 10, 2000
VENUE	Birmingham-Jefferson Civic Center
LOCATION	Birmingham, Alabama

RESULT: A chaotic ending sees multiple finishers and signature moves in succession. The Rock hits a Rock Bottom on Kurt Angle, and Stone Cold hits a Stunner on The Rock. But as Triple H steps in for a beat down on Austin, Angle regroups enough to cover a downed People's Champ to successfully defend his WWE title.

EDGE and CHRISTIAN vs. THE HARDY BOYZ vs. THE DUDLEY BOYZ

MATCH TYPE	Triangle Ladder Match
EVENT	*WrestleMania 2000*
DATE	April 2, 2000
VENUE	Arrowhead Pond
LOCATION	Anaheim, California

RESULT: After pushing Matt Hardy off a ladder and through a table, Edge and Christian grab the titles to win their first Tag Team Championship.

EDGE and CHRISTIAN vs. THE HARDY BOYZ vs. THE DUDLEY BOYZ

MATCH TYPE	TLC
EVENT	*SummerSlam*
DATE	August 27, 2000
VENUE	Raleigh Entertainment and Sports Arena
LOCATION	Raleigh, North Carolina

RESULT: With Jeff Hardy left hanging precariously by the championship title, Christian smacks Jeff down thanks to a ladder. This paves the way for Edge and Christian to retrieve their titles and retain their championships.

THE ROCK vs. TRIPLE H

MATCH TYPE	Iron Man Match
EVENT	*Judgment Day*
DATE	May 21, 2000
VENUE	Freedom Hall
LOCATION	Louisville, Kentucky

RESULT: After wrestling to a 5-5 tie, special referee Shawn Michaels is knocked out. This produces a wild ending that sees interference from the McMahons, followed by a run-in from Undertaker, who lays waste to all of the villains. HBK awakens to see Undertaker assault Triple H, thereby disqualifying The Rock and giving Triple H the 6-5 victory.

TRIPLE H vs. CACTUS JACK

MATCH TYPE	Hell in a Cell
EVENT	*No Way Out 2000*
DATE	February 27, 2000
VENUE	Hartford Civic Center
LOCATION	Hartford, Connecticut

RESULT: While fighting on the cell roof, Triple H reverses a piledriver attempt and backdrops Cactus Jack through the cell roof. Jack's fall buckles the mat, but he's still able to stand, only to be greeted by a Triple H Pedigree, enabling the Cerebral Assassin to score the pin.

TRIPLE H, X-PAC, and THE RADICALZ vs. THE ROCK, CACTUS JACK, RIKISHI, and TOO COOL

MATCH TYPE	Ten Man Tag Team Match
EVENT	*Monday Night Raw*
DATE	February 7, 2000
VENUE	Reunion Arena
LOCATION	Dallas, Texas

RESULT: In one of the best matches in the history of *Raw*—including one of the hottest crowds—Triple H hits the Pedigree on Grand Master Sexay, then Benoit climbs to the top rope to deliver the flying head-butt for the win.

EDGE and CHRISTIAN vs. THE HARDY BOYZ

MATCH TYPE	Ladder Match (Terri Invitational Tournament Finals)
EVENT	*No Mercy*
DATE	October 17, 1999
VENUE	Gund Arena
LOCATION	Cleveland, Ohio

RESULT: With $100,000 hanging from the ceiling and the managerial services of Terri Runnels going to the winner, Jeff Hardy manages to jump from ladder to ladder, fight off Edge, and grab the loot to give The New Brood the victory—not to mention, all that cash.

KURT ANGLE vs. CHRIS BENOIT

EVENT	*WrestleMania X-Seven*
DATE	April 1, 2001
VENUE	The Reliant Astrodome
LOCATION	Houston, Texas

RESULT: In a match that sees each man use his opponent's submission hold in order to make the other one tap, the mat classic ends as Angle rolls up Benoit, thanks to a handful of tights.

STONE COLD STEVE AUSTIN vs. THE ROCK

MATCH TYPE	No Disqualification
EVENT	*Backlash 1999*
DATE	April 25, 1999
VENUE	Providence Civic Center
LOCATION	Providence, Rhode Island

RESULT: With Shane McMahon serving as special guest referee, Austin hits Rock with a Stone Cold Stunner, then strikes "The Great One" with the championship title to retain the title.

STONE COLD STEVE AUSTIN vs. DUDE LOVE

EVENT	Over the Edge 1998
DATE	May 31, 1998
VENUE	Wisconsin Center Arena
LOCATION	Milwaukee, Wisconsin

RESULT: With the rules changing mid-match to No Disqualification and then to Falls Count Anywhere, Love and Austin battle each other throughout the arena. All hell breaks loose after Dude Love accidentally clobbers special referee Vince McMahon, and McMahon's goons, Gerald Brisco and Pat Patterson, try to cost Austin the victory. Eventually, after an assist from Undertaker, Austin hits the Stunner on Love and then uses McMahon's limp hand to count to three.

THE ROCK vs. KURT ANGLE

EVENT	No Way Out 2001
DATE	February 25, 2001
VENUE	Thomas and Mack Center
LOCATION	Las Vegas, Nevada

RESULT: The Rock fights off interference from Big Show and defeats Kurt Angle, thanks to an exposed turnbuckle and two Rock Bottoms, to capture the WWE Championship.

"I'm going to be your top guy, and it's not going to take me long to get there."

—The Rock

THE BIRTH OF THE GREAT ONE

When Dwayne "The Rock" Johnson first approached WWE about stepping into the ring, the former University of Miami defensive tackle wasn't shy about his ambitions.

"I remember when I first hired The Rock, he said, 'I'm going to be your top guy and it's not going to take me long to get there,'" says Jim Ross. "Being a football fan and watching the swagger of The U down in Miami, I just thought it was an extension of his college years and how he was conditioned to speak his mind. At that time, The U had a roster of very outspoken players. That was proven when all these guys went to the next level, guys like Ray Lewis, Warren Sapp, and Michael Irvin. So, what Rock says to me the day I sign him, that always stuck with me, because at the time, that was exactly the type of attitude we needed in the locker room and on our roster."

The only problem was, when Dwayne Johnson was introduced to WWE fans as poofy-haired Rocky Maivia, all of the attitude that helped the former football star stand out initially was wiped completely clean.

"My commentary about The Rock was that he was a blue chipper, but the fans were booing the hell out of him," remembers Ross. "The issue there was that the fans were ready for a change in attitude and a change in presentation. We did a traditional presentation in making the new Rocky Maivia too squeaky clean. We power washed all the edge off of him. In creative, we produced vignettes that sanitized the attitude right out of him, and the fans were tired of that traditional 'say your prayers, take your vitamins' presentation. They were sick of it."

"Rocky Maivia"
11·25·96

new costume
+
Blue colors

BASKET weave as on
original YOKE.

Preliminary costume study for the Rocky Maivia character.

"We did a traditional presentation in making the new Rocky Maivia too squeaky clean. We power washed all the edge off of him."

—Jim Ross

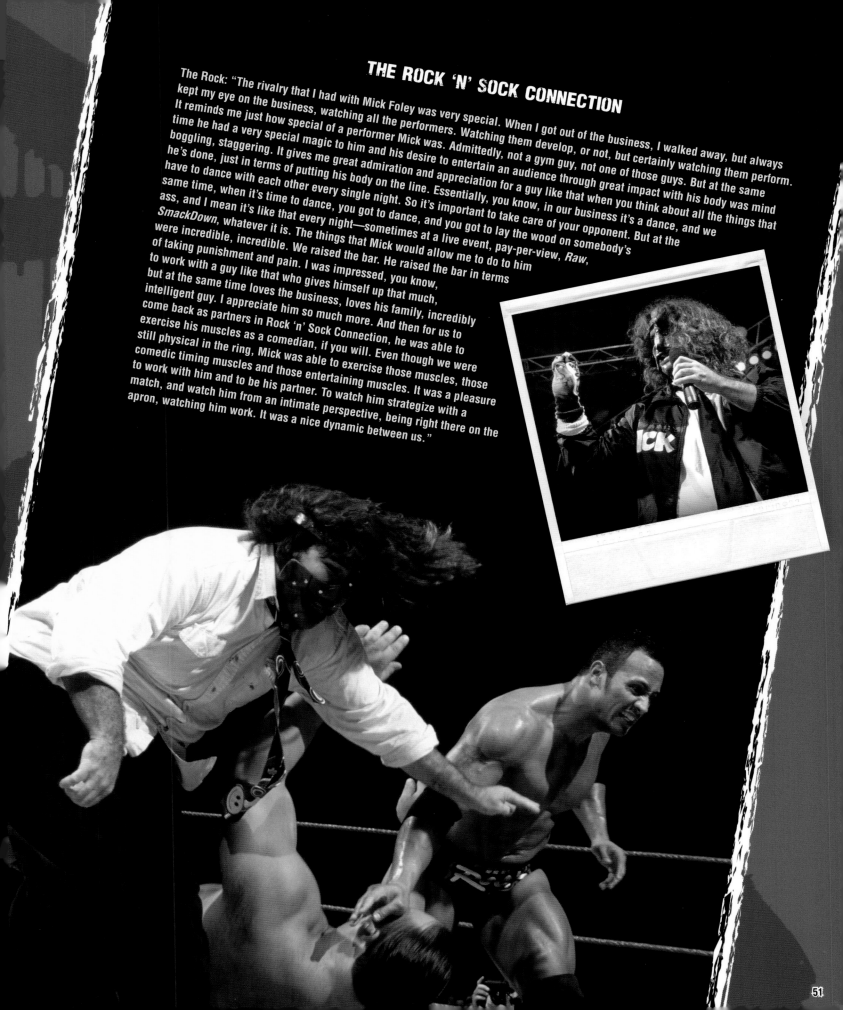

THE ROCK 'N' SOCK CONNECTION

The Rock: "The rivalry that I had with Mick Foley was very special. When I got out of the business, I walked away, but always kept my eye on the business, watching all the performers. Watching them develop, or not, but certainly watching them perform. It reminds me just how special of a performer Mick was. Admittedly, not a gym guy, not one of those guys. But at the same time he had a very special magic to him and his desire to entertain an audience through great impact with his body was mind boggling, staggering. It gives me great admiration and appreciation for a guy like that when you think about all the things that he's done, just in terms of putting his body on the line. Essentially, you know, in our business it's a dance, and we have to dance with each other every single night. So it's important to take care of your opponent. But at the same time, when it's time to dance, you got to dance, and you got to lay the wood on somebody's ass, and I mean it's like that every night—sometimes at a live event, pay-per-view, *Raw*, *SmackDown*, whatever it is. The things that Mick would allow me to do to him were incredible, incredible. We raised the bar. He raised the bar in terms of taking punishment and pain. I was impressed, you know, to work with a guy like that who gives himself up that much, but at the same time loves the business, loves his family, incredibly intelligent guy. I appreciate him so much more. And then for us to come back as partners in Rock 'n' Sock Connection, he was able to exercise his muscles as a comedian, if you will. Even though we were still physical in the ring, Mick was able to exercise those muscles, those comedic timing muscles and those entertaining muscles. It was a pleasure to work with him and to be his partner. To watch him strategize with a match, and watch him from an intimate perspective, being right there on the apron, watching him work. It was a nice dynamic between us."

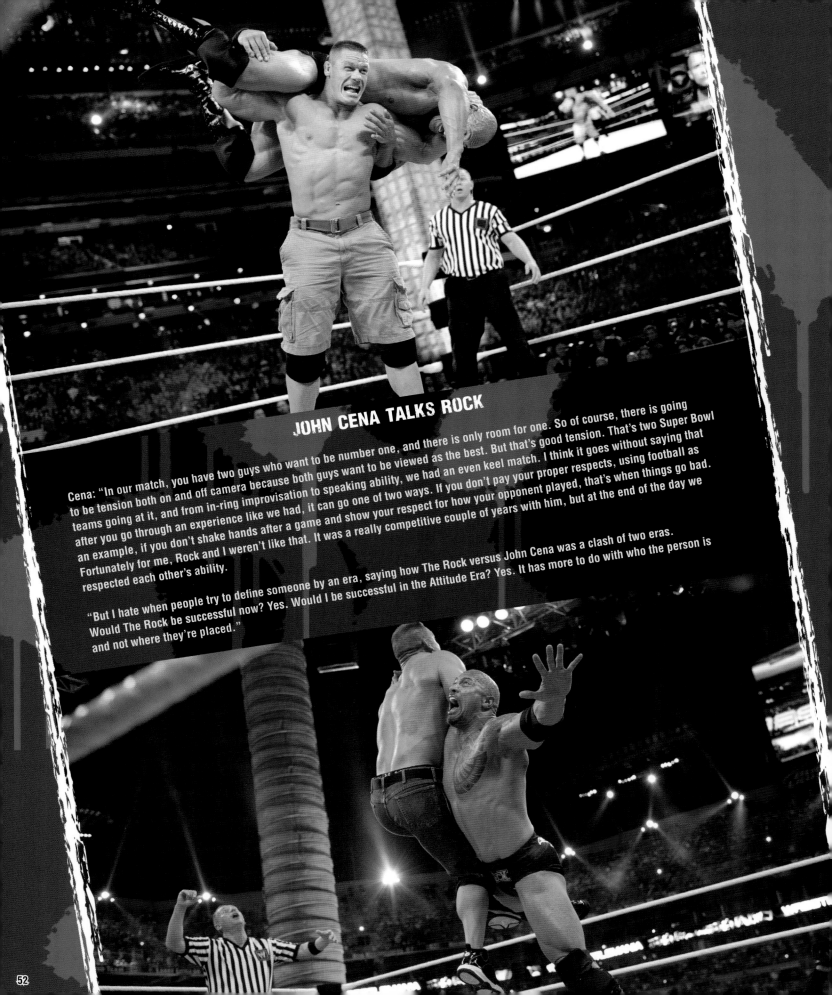

JOHN CENA TALKS ROCK

Cena: "In our match, you have two guys who want to be number one, and there is only room for one. So of course, there is going to be tension both on and off camera because both guys want to be viewed as the best. But that's good tension. That's two Super Bowl teams going at it, and from in-ring improvisation to speaking ability, we had an even keel match. I think it goes without saying that after you go through an experience like we had, it can go one of two ways. If you don't pay your proper respects, using football as an example, if you don't shake hands after a game and show your respect for how your opponent played, that's when things go bad. Fortunately for me, Rock and I weren't like that. It was a really competitive couple of years with him, but at the end of the day we respected each other's ability.

"But I hate when people try to define someone by an era, saying how The Rock versus John Cena was a clash of two eras. Would The Rock be successful now? Yes. Would I be successful in the Attitude Era? Yes. It has more to do with who the person is and not where they're placed."

"They'd already been there, seen it, and got the t-shirt, but it wasn't Rock's fault. Rock executed the plan perfectly; we just gave him the wrong game plan of who we wanted him to be. We went traditional, gave him all of these wonderful qualities, which he actually had. He was a third generation star, he played on a national championship football team at a major program … but the people couldn't care less. They wanted some attitude. They wanted some swag. Rock had all that, but we suppressed it." It wasn't long before chants of "Rocky Sucks!" were followed by signs like "Die Rocky Die," and WWE creative realized they needed to flip the script.

"If you're not authentic, then you're done," says The Rock. "Fans see through that. Fans immediately see … it's just like a performer or an actor. If you're phoning it in, fans can see it. If you're in the ring and you're doing things, you're going through the motions, and you're kind of phoning your performance in, and you're not being authentic, being real, and coming from your heart, then they see through that.

"And then, eventually, eventually, you find yourself in trouble. So, that's what happened with my character, because I was told, 'Listen, when you go out there, you go and smile.' 'Okay, but I'm going to lose tonight.' 'Yeah, but you're happy to be here.' And I would bump up against that.

Emotionally, I would bump up against it, because I would lose, and yet I would still have to carry this smile back to the locker room. And that drove fans crazy, because that's bullshit, and they can see through it. They saw through it, and they were like … that's when they became visceral, and basically, 'You're full of shit.' And, at that time, I was [full of shit], because I wasn't coming from a real place and I was doing what I was told."

Says Ross, "The crowd declared what they perceived him to be, and that was not a fan favorite, but a villain. We were trying to build the next big fan favorite, but what we ended up with was a major villain."

After sitting out with a knee injury, Rocky Maivia was reintroduced as the latest member of Farooq's Nation of Domination, grabbing the mic and giving fans a taste of the character that would go on to become the most electrifying man in sports-entertainment history.

"I was just able to be authentic," remembers Rock. And it was that authenticity that shot the Superstar straight up the card and eventually to the main event, even becoming the youngest WWE Champion at the time.

"That shit was sweet," laughs Rock. "I grew up in the business. I love the business. So, you work your ass off to reach a certain point. You reach the proverbial brass ring. You work your ass off, and you have the opportunity to become 'the guy,' the World Champion of the company, the face of the company. It's an exciting time. That was really, really an exciting time, because things had begun to happen so quickly. I was a heel first, and through just my nature, my desire to entertain ... like even when I became a heel and I was in the Nation, became the leader of the Nation, and then started to break off, my goal was just to entertain the fans. I didn't want to be the loudest. I didn't want to be the biggest. But I did want to be the best, and I did want to be the most entertaining. I wanted to go into every performance, whether it was on the microphone, whether it was the ring, without any inhibition. And I always thought there is nothing that I won't try. I'm going to try it and see if it sticks. And if it does, great; if it doesn't, great."

The Rock was so authentic, so true to his character, that the man who was so hated as a face that he was forced to become a "villain" became arguably the second most popular character on the card. That authenticity, that personality, on display on TV and on the mic led The Rock to become The People's Champion. And now, the man with the raised eyebrow and People's Elbow was hearing the crowd respond at a volume level previously reserved only for Stone Cold.

"If you're not authentic, then you're done."

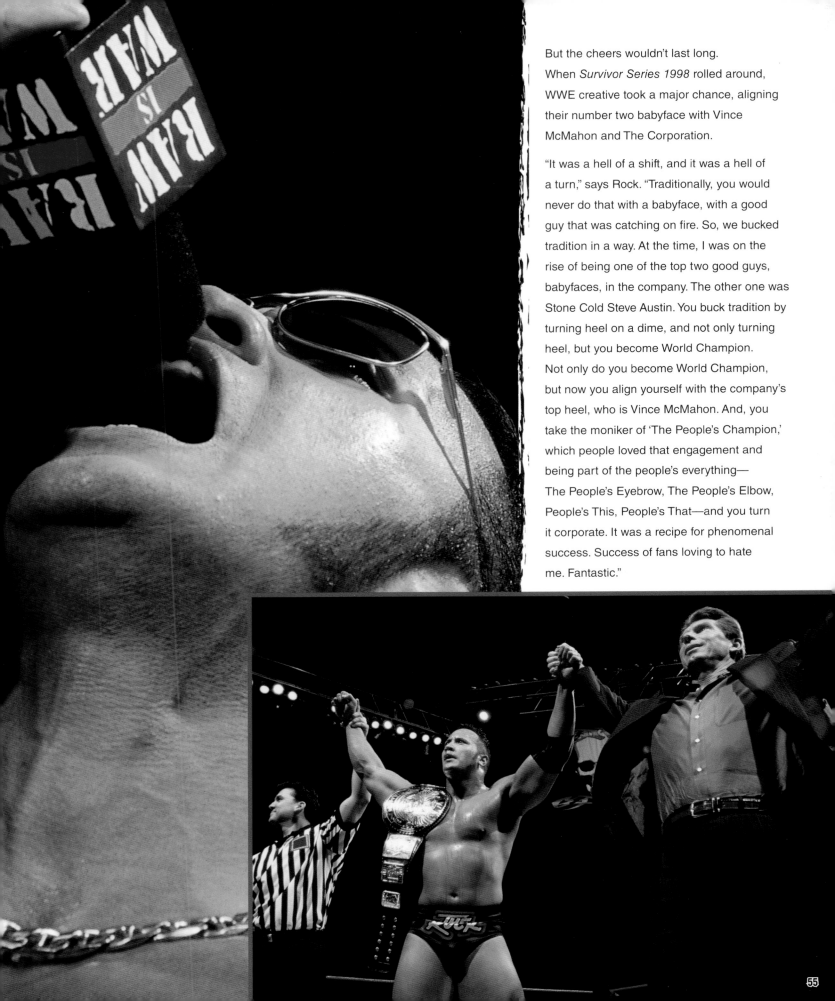

But the cheers wouldn't last long. When *Survivor Series 1998* rolled around, WWE creative took a major chance, aligning their number two babyface with Vince McMahon and The Corporation.

"It was a hell of a shift, and it was a hell of a turn," says Rock. "Traditionally, you would never do that with a babyface, with a good guy that was catching on fire. So, we bucked tradition in a way. At the time, I was on the rise of being one of the top two good guys, babyfaces, in the company. The other one was Stone Cold Steve Austin. You buck tradition by turning heel on a dime, and not only turning heel, but you become World Champion. Not only do you become World Champion, but now you align yourself with the company's top heel, who is Vince McMahon. And, you take the moniker of 'The People's Champion,' which people loved that engagement and being part of the people's everything— The People's Eyebrow, The People's Elbow, People's This, People's That—and you turn it corporate. It was a recipe for phenomenal success. Success of fans loving to hate me. Fantastic."

FAMILY TRADITIONS

The Rock: "Growing up in a family of wrestling was, of course, incredibly influential to me, because I fell in love with the business. At three, four years old, I was at the matches. I just, I remember being four years old in Dallas at the Sportatorium when the Von Erichs ran it. Fritz Von Erich was the promoter at the time. My dad was there so, I mean, my memories are strong. My love and the passion for the business are very strong.

"So, I grew up loving wrestling. I grew up on the road. At that time, there were territories all across the country, so I was constantly moving about every year, year and a half. Growing up in the business and having a love and an affinity for the business made it easy for me. Once I recognized that my football career came to an end, and I wanted to end that chapter in my life, well, what's the next chapter? What's the next challenge? That next chapter and challenge is going to be, I think, what my first love is. And I say, 'I think,' because at that time, when I decided to start training for wrestling, I didn't know. I didn't know if I was going to be good. You just never know, because life is so unpredictable, and this world of professional wrestling, the WWE, was so incredibly unpredictable. But I did think, at that time, that I might have had something to offer."

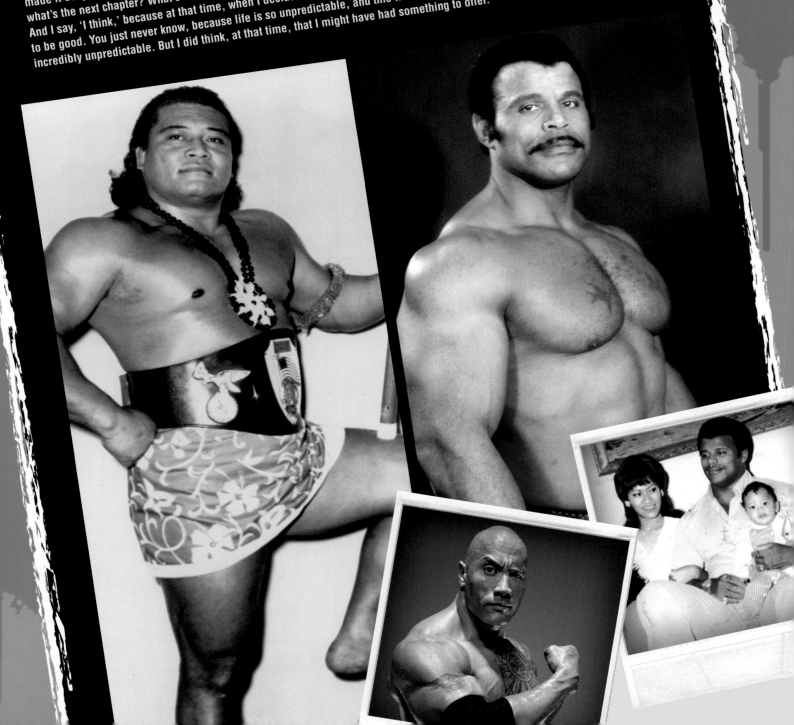

56

The turn not only helped elevate The Rock to the company's number one heel Superstar, but also helped lead to the rivalry that would go on to define the Attitude Era: The Rock versus Stone Cold Steve Austin.

"I love Steve. And I'm so grateful of not only the friendship that we have today, the friendship we had then, but also, at that time, the company was trendsetting and groundbreaking, and we were ushering in this incredible era. So, it was important to me that I was the one leading the pack," says Rock. "I didn't want to be second when I knew first was available. And Steve Austin sure didn't want to be second when he knew first was available.

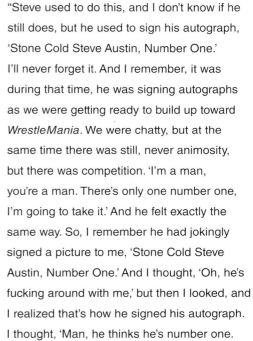

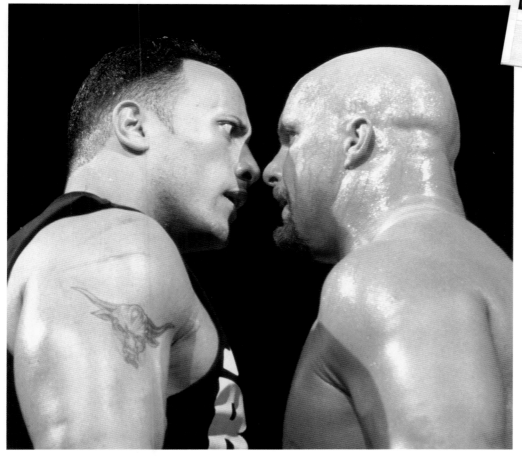

"Steve used to do this, and I don't know if he still does, but he used to sign his autograph, 'Stone Cold Steve Austin, Number One.' I'll never forget it. And I remember, it was during that time, he was signing autographs as we were getting ready to build up toward *WrestleMania*. We were chatty, but at the same time there was still, never animosity, but there was competition. 'I'm a man, you're a man. There's only one number one, I'm going to take it.' And he felt exactly the same way. So, I remember he had jokingly signed a picture to me, 'Stone Cold Steve Austin, Number One.' And I thought, 'Oh, he's fucking around with me,' but then I looked, and I realized that's how he signed his autograph. I thought, 'Man, he thinks he's number one. Okay.' It was just a small thing. As a performer, as an athlete, as a man, I can appreciate that. I appreciate that stamp, I'm number one, but it bugged me. I was like, 'Shit, one day I'm going to write number one. In order for that to happen, I've got to beat him.'

THE ROCK VS. TRIPLE H

The Rock: "[Triple H] was my first big rivalry, and it was for the Intercontinental Title. He was Hunter Hearst-Helmsley, a blue blood. I was Rocky Maivia, and I was wearing my white and my blue and my happy face, so I think we both felt at that time that there was more. We were lions. We were lions who were hungry for more. We worked our asses off, and I thought we had really good matches in the beginning. But then, we were fortunate enough to recognize that what we were doing just wasn't working in terms of our characters. When you strip it all down, you can over-intellectualize it. At the end of the day, the shit didn't work because it wasn't real, it wasn't authentic. He then became real. He became authentic. I became real and became authentic. And out of that we had these incredible rivalries.

"I enjoyed working with him, physically working with him, probably more than anybody else in WWE because he was a hell of an athlete. He is. He's a hell of an athlete and loved, still loves, the business of wrestling, professional wrestling. When you work with someone who just loves it so much ... And look, there's something about Triple H that I admire, because he is a no-nonsense guy, all about the business. Often times when you're in a position like that, when you're in a position of success, a lot of guys are going to try to dog you, they're going to try to talk shit about you. It happens to everybody. Anybody that has any semblance of success, it just happens. And he was one of those guys that still stayed steadfast in his beliefs. 'This is what I believe. This is what I want to do. This is who I am.' He stayed steadfast in that. If it was anybody talking shit, not only did he overcome it, but the guy became one of the greatest performers in the history of the WWE. And still, to this day, to be able to go out, for example, at *WrestleMania 27* and have the best match of the night, have one of the best matches ever. Very, very impressive. Loved working with him."

Old rivals share a tense exchange at WrestleMania XXVII.

"And then we went to *WrestleMania* that first time, and he beat me, so he had taken number one. Even Stone Cold Steve Austin writing, 'Stone Cold, Number One,' doing little things like that, which now I can appreciate that he did that, but that competition was strong. And what's interesting, it wound up being arguably the greatest rivalry in the history of WWE. And that's saying something with all these incredible rivalries." A rivalry that started with tension between the two performers, both in and out of the ring.

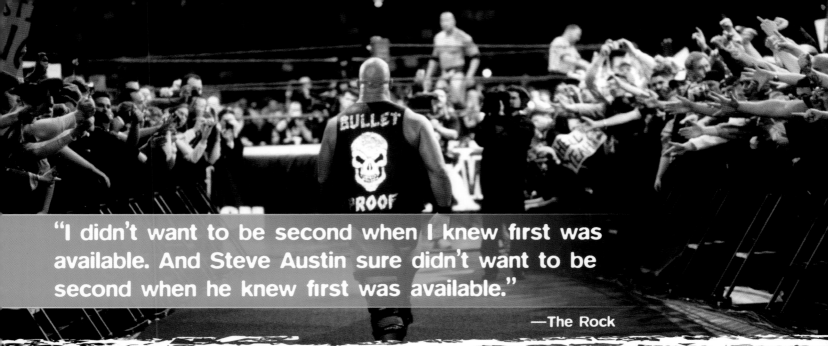

"If you look back, look over the years, in our rivalry, there was tension, but it was great tension in the beginning, because he didn't know me, I didn't know him," says Rock. "He didn't trust me. And it's not that I didn't trust him; I felt, 'You couldn't do anything to hurt me.' I didn't mean physically, I didn't mean like a fight, but I know the type of guy that I am. I'm not going to fuck you over in any way; I'm a straight up guy. But he's the same way. He was just a little bit more reluctant. So, you see that tension in the beginning.

"Then you see it start to get peeled away when he started to trust me, and we started to trust each other as performers, too, because he was coming back from an injury that could have been career ending for him. So, in the ring, he started trusting me more, which then made our matches that much better. And, as a performer, in terms of ego, checking ego at the door, he knew that he could trust me with that, too. Because we would have these performances and these monologues, where he knew that I said, 'Man, you can say anything, anything that you want. Anything. I have no ego.

And then I'll come back for you, and we'll have fun. It'll be fun for the audience.'" That fun included everything from the main event spot at *WrestleMania* to The Rock throwing Austin off of a Detroit bridge.

Adds Ross, "We saw a rivalry between two hot Superstars who helped push each other to greatness, and these two men helped define the Attitude Era unlike any other."

THE PEOPLE'S STRUDEL

Fans remember The People's Eyebrow, The People's Elbow, and The People's Champion, but one of the funniest Rock segments brought the people to a whole new place. Here's what The Rock said to Lilian Garcia in one of his frequent attempts to make the beautiful ring announcer blush:

"Whoa-whoa-whoa-whoa-whoa. Lilian. Lilian. You need to let your feelings go. The Rock knows you have feelings for him. The Rock knows that you think about The Rock. The Rock knows that you get that funny feeling in the bottom of your stomach, Lilian. The Rock knows that each and every single time you go right out there in the middle of The People's ring and you ring announce, you think about The Rock looking at you. Admit it, Lilian, that you go to bed every single night dreaming about marrying The Rock. Dreaming of one day to become Mrs. Lilian 'Rockcia'. Admit it, Lilian, you get wet ... with perspiration, standing this close to The Rock. Now, Lilian, The Rock knows how you feel about pie. But how do you feel about strudel? Lilian, would you like to try some of The Rock's strudel?"

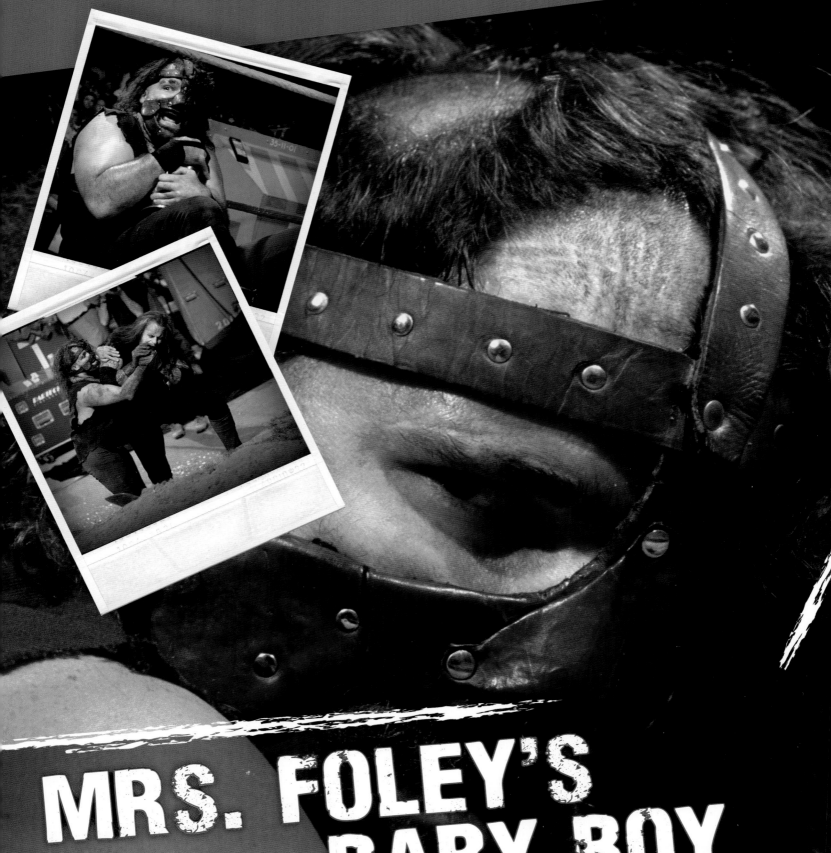

MRS. FOLEY'S BABY BOY

When WWE signed hardcore legend Mick Foley to transform into the role of Mankind back in 1996, the words "future World Champion" were not in the contract, let alone on anyone's mind.

"Mick Foley was not a 5-star, highly regarded recruit," says Jim Ross. "I thought he had untapped talent and would match up very well working with Undertaker. With Undertaker, we had a 7-foot fan favorite. When you have a 7-foot fan favorite, you have to be very selective with the villain he's paired with because it's very difficult, if you're a fan, to show empathy for a hero when he's 7-feet, 300 pounds. Why should I feel sorry for the big guy? Sure, he's getting beat up, but he's bigger than his opponent. The thing about Foley is that he's a big guy. He's 6' 4", 300 pounds plus, and he could talk, so I was reluctantly given the blessing to hire him."

Hiring Foley led to not only a worthy opponent for Undertaker, but one of the Attitude Era's signature moments, *Hell in a Cell*.

"... In some ways, the latter-day Mankind was the anti-Attitude Era guy. But I still had the credentials to back it up."

—Mick Foley

> "As God as my witness, he is broken in half. Somebody stop the damn match."
>
> —Jim Ross

JIM ROSS ON "THE CALL"

"Looking back at it, it was probably one of the most memorable moments of the Attitude Era. I'm not condoning it, but as a broadcaster, I had no idea it was going to occur. That call, which was 16 years ago, I still get that call every day on Twitter: 'As God as my witness, he's been broken in half. Somebody stop the damn match.' People randomly tweet those words to me every day. Certainly it was a spectacular, high-risk moment that should never be attempted or replicated again. It was breathtaking. I never played the role of a wrestling announcer. It's not a role I was cast in. Even though it's a theatrical presentation and everybody has a role, the guys who are best at their roles are the ones who are most naturally placed in their position. I'm not an actor, and McMahon has told me that to my face. He told me, 'You're a horrible actor, but, man, do you have great instincts.' So when we did TV, the less I knew about what was going on, the better I was. If there were little nuances that the producers felt I needed to be made aware of, that's one thing, but they knew I wanted to know as little as possible about what was going to happen. That way, I could react naturally, organically, and in a real way."

"I get asked all the time," says Ross, "what's the best match I ever called in the Attitude Era. That's a tough one because we had some guys who really loved to bring it on game day and steal the show, but the most memorable match I ever called was *Hell in a Cell* in Pittsburgh. The reason it's the most memorable is because people refuse to forget it. This match gets brought up all the time, not just by fans, but by sites lifting the commentary and putting it over video of everything from NBA dunks to UFC knockouts. Somebody got the idea to put the commentary over a huge tackle by Jadeveon Clowney a couple of years ago and the video went viral, so now the audio seems to pop up in more and more places. The irony is a lot of the younger fans weren't even around 16 years ago, so a lot of them are seeing it for the first time on WWE Network or on YouTube, so now it's seeping into their consciousness."

The match included two of the most death-defying stunts ever performed in a WWE ring, one resulting in Foley's teeth getting lodged in his nose, with thousands of thumbtacks providing the exclamation point for the eye-popping spectacle.

"I had an emotional investment in the man that I hired," says Ross. "Then, as an announcer, I had an emotional investment in the match. So seeing a human being who I had engaged in dialogue and who I was managing in my department go flying off the top of the cell 18 to 20 feet through a wooden table, it's not the best thing you want to see your talent do. They're not helping you when they're hurt. You don't want to see anybody get hurt. Just like any other sport, you want to see them stay in the game. How is this guy going to stay in the game or ever be the same after doing that? So part of my call was fear, part of my call was frustration, part of my call was anger. There was a gambit of emotions that ran through me during that interval. It's a moment, it's a call, that will live forever."

While replays of the match live on anytime WWE fans want to see the "extreme," Mick Foley himself didn't realize the match's true meaning until much later.

"It's funny, but at the time that *Hell in a Cell* took place, and even in the immediate aftermath, it didn't seem there was any historical significance for the company, or for me," says Foley. "It wasn't something that was played up much. After the match, I remember Shawn Michaels coming back at a time when he wasn't on the show very often. He came back and said, 'Hey, if nobody else is going to talk about it, I might as well mention it.'"

"It was an amazing event, but largely forgotten," continues Foley. "It was like a groundswell though. It was a slow building thing. Immediately after that match, I specifically thought my career was in the doldrums. What I did not know is that when it happened, Kevin Sullivan who was one of the members of the booking committee for WCW specifically said, 'That's it, brother. The fight is over. They just won the war. It's over. Pack it up. Go home. It's over.' I didn't get that feeling at all, but looking back at it, I think that the moment, or a few of those moments, have gone on to define for some people what was most outrageous, right or wrong, about the Attitude Era."

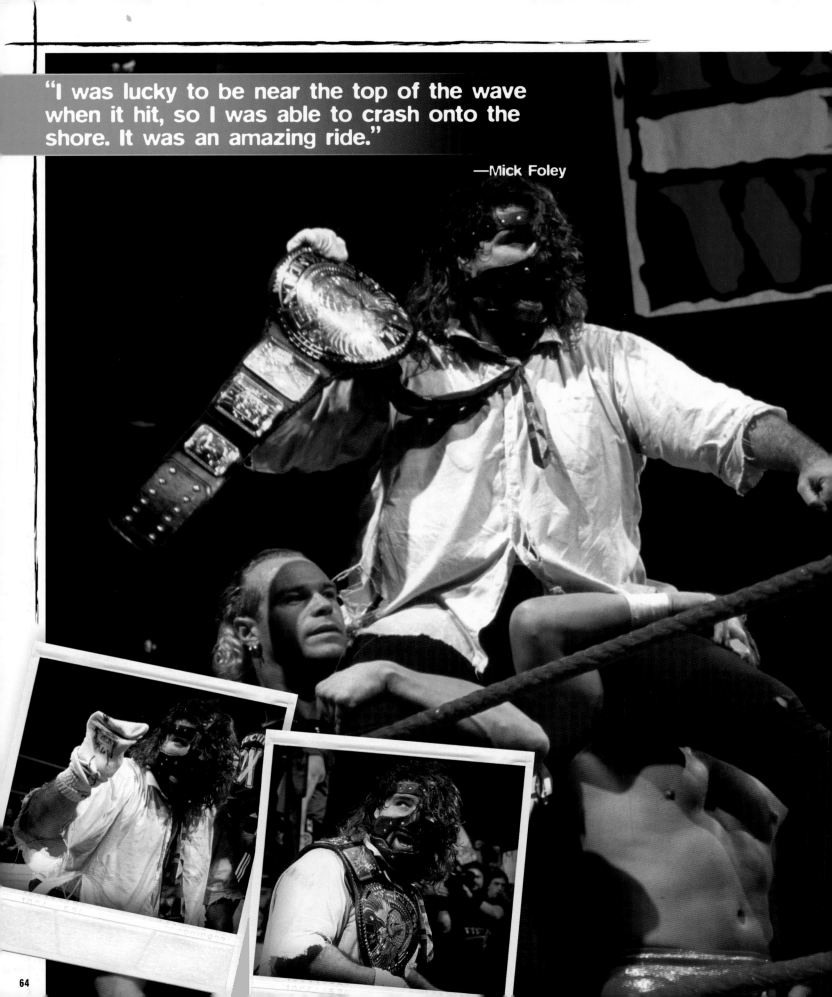

"I was lucky to be near the top of the wave when it hit, so I was able to crash onto the shore. It was an amazing ride."

—Mick Foley

64

The match helped turn Foley from cult hero to top-tier Superstar. Celebrated and historic rivalries ensued with everyone from The Rock and Stone Cold Steve Austin to Triple H and The Corporation.

But Foley's greatest night, the night nobody saw coming, was December 29, 1998. Mankind defeated The Rock on *Monday Night Raw* to capture his first of three WWE World Heavyweight Championships. What's most remembered about that night, however, isn't necessarily that Foley won or how he won, but the fact that WCW announcer Tony Schiavone gave away the results live on *Nitro* with the infamous line: "That's gonna put some butts in the seats." This caused hundreds of thousands of WCW viewers to change the channel to see how Foley's underdog story played out, creating a major shift (and victory) toward WWE in the Monday Night War.

What Schiavone and WCW didn't realize is just how beloved a character Foley had become to fans. Through a combination of insane bumps, timely comedy, and a sock puppet used to apply his Mandible Claw finishing hold (Mr. Socko!), Foley had truly broken out as one of the top players of this or any era.

"I'm sure my contributions have been somewhat exaggerated," says Foley. "I was lucky to be near the top of the wave when it hit, so I was able to crash onto the shore. It was an amazing ride. But had it not been for the guys that had been responsible for the wave—mainly Stone Cold, and then later The Rock—no one would have remembered that I was near it. I benefitted from being around some great guys. I still to this day feel that I was a supporting actor who stole some scenes. But I was never the lead guy. If people want to disagree with me, they can feel free to, but I was possibly the most overrated Superstar of the Attitude Era, yeah!"

And even when Foley could no longer bring it in the ring like he once did, the Superstar is proud he was still able to offer his own brand of comedy to *Raw*.

"I think my fondest memory of the Attitude Era was just when I realized that I couldn't physically do some of the things that I had done for a long time, and that I had to find a different way to connect with the audience," says Foley. "That ended up being humor. Even though a lot of our audience will remember me for *Hell in a Cell*, or for an extreme match with Triple H or with Stone Cold, I think just as many will look back at the moments that I spent with The Rock. Not just the 'This is Your Life' skit, but also some great moments with The Rock and Al Snow. And great moments with Christian and Edge, or Kurt Angle, when I was the Commissioner. People might say, 'You know what? He was able to find a way, even when his body was giving out on him, to connect with our audience and become a big part of the Attitude Era. Even when what he was doing was in the face of what was making Attitude cool.'"

"It was just me realizing, 'Not everybody that was a part of the Attitude Era was nearly as cool as we were thinking them to be.' So, in some ways, the latter-day Mankind was the anti-Attitude Era guy. But I still had the credentials to back it up. I was just glad that I was able to make people laugh and gasp in equal pleasure."

"If people want to disagree with me, they can feel free to, but I was possibly the most overrated Superstar of the Attitude Era, yeah!"

—Mick Foley

THIS IS YOUR LIFE

While Foley will be remembered for comedy pieces ranging from Mr. McMahon's hospital room to classic one-liners at the expense of Al Snow, it's Foley's "This is Your Life" skit with The Rock that goes down as generating the most laughs per minute of possibly any skit in WWE history.

"When Rock and I did the 'This is Your Life' segment, behind the scenes, I guess Mr. McMahon was furious because we were allotted 14 minutes for a segment on live television, and we went 26," laughs Foley. "26 minutes! And, if you watch it back, the names that I was talking about were not the names that were showing up on the screens. When I'd say, 'Here's your teacher, Betty Griffith,' or 'Everett Hart' was the name of his coach, which happened to be the name of a high school coach that I played for, the names were completely different."

"There was no script. It was just: The Rock would say something, he'd do something, and then I'd say something. Nobody knew what was going to happen. He obviously was off to the races and in great form. But from Mr. McMahon's perspective backstage, this was a live show on national television that was running really long and wasn't going all that well."

"It wasn't until the next day when The Rock tapped me on the shoulder and said, 'Did you hear about the ratings?' I think it was like an 8.4, something just ridiculous. It was so extreme that if it happened in the current day of texting or tweeting, it may be easy to explain, but the only way I can explain it is to say hundreds of thousands of people had to have actually been on their telephones, calling up friends who were not even watching WCW, saying, 'You have to look at what's on WWE.' Sure a lot of WCW shifted over, but those alone can't explain the huge upsurge. It was just this moment that caught people that they loved and enjoyed and think of with great fondness. I'm happy I was a part of it."

THREE FACES OF FOLEY

During Mick Foley's Attitude Era run, he not only introduced the WWE world to Mankind, but he also played the roles of flower-power hippie Dude Love and the barbed-wire eating Cactus Jack. *Royal Rumble* 1998 even saw all three characters compete in the same match.

Dude Love

Mankind

Cactus Jack

TWO SIDES OF THE FALL

No question, Mick Foley's fall from the cell is one of the craziest moments ever seen in WWE, but was it worth the risk? John Cena and The Miz offer different takes:

JOHN CENA:

"It's something that you look back on now, and as a 12-year veteran, I think how ridiculous it was. The setup could've caused a horrible accident that potentially could have cost him his life. It was him being brave, but it's not something anybody should ever do or try again because of the ridiculous risk involved."

THE MIZ:

"*Hell in a Cell* is where Mick Foley got put on the map. I'll never forget where I was when Undertaker threw Mankind off of the cage and through the announcer's desk. I was sitting in my living room with my buddies, and we were all goofing around and talking. But then we see them go to the top of the cage, and it was silence. He got thrown off the top of the cage, and we were all like, 'Oh my god! There is no way that is not real.' How do you stage a guy getting thrown off a steel cage? You just can't. We thought there was no way this guy could go on. We didn't even know if he was still alive. But then all of a sudden he gets up, he climbs to the top of the cage again, and he gets chokeslammed through the roof of the cage! I'll never forget seeing the tooth in his nose. All I could think was, 'This guy is absolutely nuts. He's absolutely crazy.' And I couldn't wait to see what he'd do next. The guy would do anything. He just did not absorb pain. He's like a superhero."

DIVA$

WWE Hall of Famer Trish Stratus still remembers the day she signed with WWE and showed up to watch a live pay-per-view event from behind the scenes. Diva action inside the ring included everything from skimpy outfits to no outfits at all.

"There was a pool, there were bikinis, and there was a moment when Terri Runnels pulled The Kat's top off," laughs Stratus as she recalls the outlandish, over-the-top Diva days of the Attitude Era. "I remember looking at my husband and going, 'Ewww, this isn't a good direction.'

"I was scared that this was the type of stuff they wanted me to do. But I was an athlete, so I made the conscious decision when I joined WWE to craft my career around being an athlete. I understood I needed to flaunt sexiness, which was difficult for me because it's not my natural thing, but I wanted to be remembered for my athleticism and what I could do in the ring."

And Stratus did just that, beginning her legendary career as a valet for Test and Albert (T&A), then quickly transitioning into her role as one of the most dominant Divas ever to lace up a pair of boots.

"In the Attitude Era, the women were given the same opportunity to go out there and compete with the boys," says Stratus. "As a Diva, I got a chance to tag team with The Rock and go against Vince McMahon and Kurt Angle. That type of thing just doesn't happen today. I even tag teamed with Triple H to go against Lita and The Rock. When have you ever seen women in these types of matches?

"In the Attitude Era, women were considered equal to the guys. We were all just characters, and every character was given the opportunity to compete. I was Powerbombed through a table by Bubba Ray Dudley, I was Chokeslammed over the top rope by Big Show, I was Chokeslammed by Kane. All of these things did wonders to not only build up my credibility as a character, but as a performer, proving to everyone backstage that I was willing to take these types of chances."

But Stratus wasn't the only Diva lighting it up inside the ring, as the Attitude Era also saw breakout performances by Chyna (first woman to enter the *Royal Rumble*, first female Intercontinental Champion), as well as the debut of high-flying Hall of Famer Lita.

"The best thing about the Attitude Era was, if you had an idea, everyone was up for trying it to see if it worked, whether you were The Rock or a Diva," says Lita. "Women had a lot of really unique roles and were seen in ways like never before on TV. When I first got to WWE, the women that were there were making an impact because their characters were just larger than life. To have Luna Vachon with the Oddities, she didn't look or act like anyone else. Then you had Chyna, who was so huge, she was the definition of larger than life. Sable was this blonde bombshell walking out with handprints on her boobs. These were the images I had of the women when I started my career with WWE. This was the pinnacle time in sports-entertainment."

This period even saw Lita get physically involved in the brutal TLC Matches alongside Matt and Jeff Hardy as a member of Team Xtreme. "The TLC Matches were really groundbreaking," says Lita. "From Shawn Michaels versus Razor Ramon's classic Ladder Match, how do you one-up it? Throw tables in the mix. It was that ECW mentality of anything goes, and there was a heightened level of danger in these matches. Knowing what was going to happen, it was really hard to react. When Edge or Christian went through a table, as a valet for Team Xtreme, I should've been like, 'Screw you guys, you just went through a table.' But what I was really thinking was, 'Did he land safely? Do I see any blood?' These are my friends out there, and I wanted everybody to be as safe as they possibly could. It was quite an honor and privilege to be the only woman in that TLC mix. The whole experience was just magical."

Adds Stratus, "In the Attitude Era, you had a handful of girls who were fully competent and confident in the ring. Before us, the Diva's skill set was a little girly. It was almost like play wrestling. They were just doing moves, but there was no psychology. Everyone was really pretty in the ring, but the matches were not. In the Attitude Era, that was the first time where the girls were not only gorgeous, but they could really bring it in the ring. We were at the point back then where every girl, just like the guys, had her own move set. It's just like the video game—you have to have your own move set, you can't use somebody else's moves. You don't want everybody doing tilt-a-whirls out there. You don't want everybody out there doing Moonsaults because that's Lita's move. You need to protect these moves as being something special.

"We wanted to stand out. We wanted to be looked at as unique characters. And in the Attitude Era, females were finally just as fierce inside the ring as out."

TRISH
STRATUS

"In the Attitude Era, that was the first time where the girls were not only gorgeous, but they could really bring it in the ring."

—Trish Stratus

LITA

FABULOUS MOOLAH

"It was quite an honor and privilege to be the only woman in that TLC mix. The whole experience was just magical."

MAE
YOUNG

SABLE

DIVAS DO PLAYBOY

In 1999, sexy Sable became the first WWE Diva to pose nude for *Playboy* magazine, but she was far from the last, as Chyna and Torrie Wilson also posed. These Divas laid the groundwork for Candice Michelle, Ashley Massaro, Maria, and Christy Hemme to later join Hugh Hefner's list of cover girls.

THE KAT

JACQUELINE

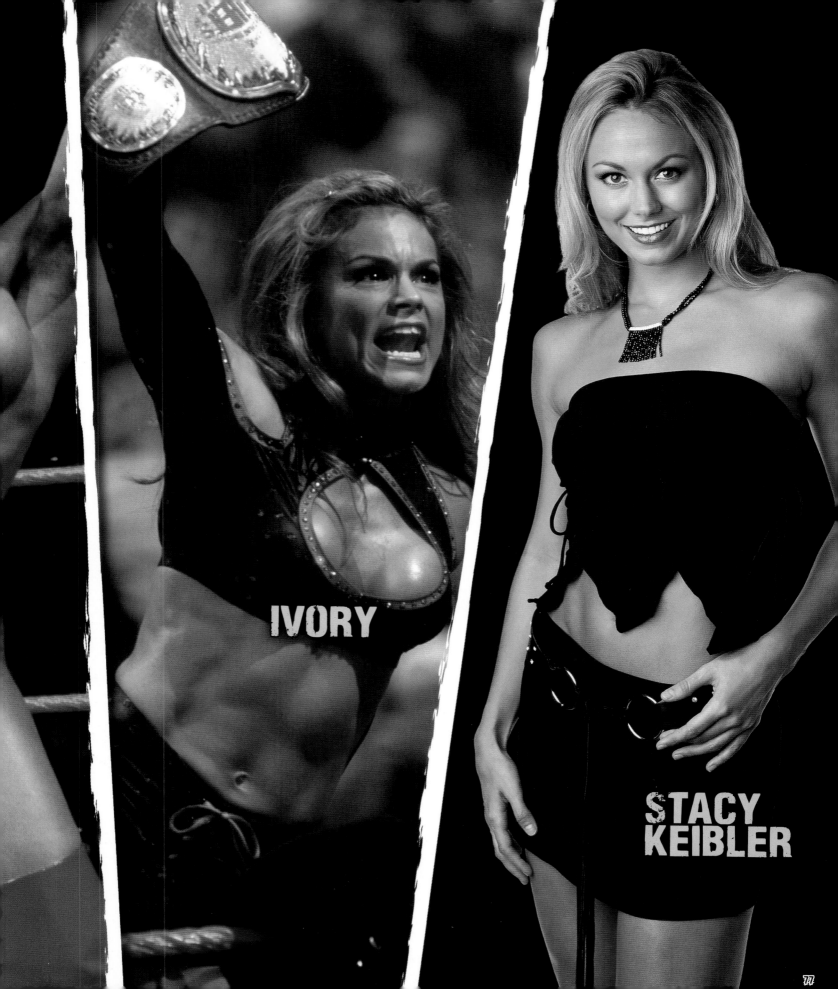

IVORY

STACY
KEIBLER

TORRIE
WILSON

LUNA VACHON

MOLLY
HOLLY

KISS OF DEATH

Prior to the PG era, Divas seemed to be down to do anything on air, but Stratus says that refusing to do a segment behind the scenes once cost her the title. "Stephanie (McMahon) wanted me to crawl on Torrie and kiss her," explains Stratus. "I said I'd kiss her on the cheek, but Stephanie didn't think that was sexy enough. She wanted me to kiss her on the lips. I didn't feel like I was in a position to say no, so I kept saying I'd do it, but just not with a sexy kiss on the lips. That didn't go so well, and Stacy (Keibler) ended up doing it instead. That was just too risqué for me. The thing is, Mickie and I kissed, I kissed Lita, so kissing isn't the thing; it's about the storyline. I'll do anything, including barking like a dog if it makes sense for my character. And at that point, my character had nothing to do with Torrie, so I didn't think she would kiss her. My character wasn't built around being this sexy person, and I was so passionate about my character, I just didn't think it made sense for me. If Torrie and I were in a tag team and we kissed to distract our opponents or pull the wool over some guy's eyes, I'd be all for it. But as a standalone moment, it just didn't make sense.

"This segment was filmed on a Tuesday for *SmackDown*. I was the champion, so I went home, came to the next show on Monday, and I lost the title clean to Jazz. So, was I being punished? Who knows? I was never told that's why I lost, but it was a little strange that *WrestleMania* in my hometown of Toronto was coming up, and all of a sudden, I wasn't going in as champion. Eventually, I got the title back, so it was all good, but I still stand by my decision at the time."

STEPHANIE MCMAHON

TRISH GOES THROUGH A TABLE

"When T&A first started to compete with the Dudleys, I knew right then that I would be going through a table at some point," says Stratus. "Bubba had already thrown everybody from Terri Runnels to Mae Young through a table, so I was all on board. I was brand new at the time, so this was a great way for the fans to get to know T&A and to get to know me. It was great for character development. The fact that I could show fans that I was able to put my body on the line really meant a lot. Bubba told me, 'You can do it the easy way, or you can take the table.' I took the table. I wanted to do it the hard way. I trusted him and I knew he would take care of me. It was this amazing, euphoric feeling to go through the table, and the crowd really went crazy when it happened."

CHYNA

80

DEBRA

MARLENA

SHOW ME YOUR PUPPIES!

PUPPIES

Not only did Jerry "The King" Lawler coin the term "puppies" as he ogled the lovely Divas from ringside, his euphemism perfectly targeted the college-aged fans that WWE courted at the time. The gimmick caught on, as scores of enthusiastic onlookers often chanted, "we want puppies!"

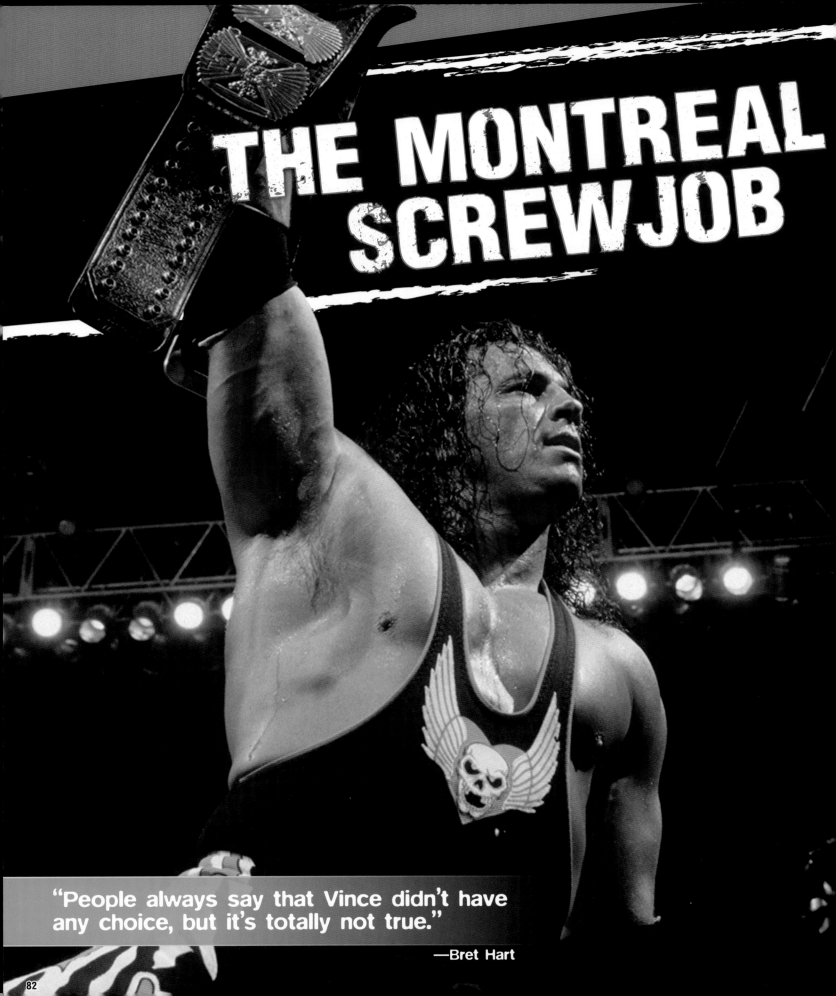

THE MONTREAL SCREWJOB

"People always say that Vince didn't have any choice, but it's totally not true."

—Bret Hart

Bret Hart walked into Montreal's Molson Centre thinking he was leaving the arena with his WWE Championship. Vince McMahon had other plans.

This was *Survivor Series 1997*, and the economic fate of WWE hung in the balance. Earlier that year, the struggling organization signed Hart, a true legend and one of the most popular performers on their roster, to a 20-year, multimillion dollar contract that owner Vince McMahon was coming to realize the company couldn't afford. So McMahon added an out-clause to Hart's new contract, enabling The Excellence of Execution to be signed by rival WCW.

"I allowed Bret to be stolen by WCW and Eric Bischoff," says McMahon. "I had determined that Bret was the last star we had that Turner did not have. And I was like, I really need to hold onto Bret, so we came up with this contract with Bret and tried to compete with WCW and it was—again, they had a bigger checkbook. So I made a deal that I had regretted. And I don't know, we were a couple months into it and I said, 'Bret, look—we have to work something out here. I can't continue on like this. We live in the real world; they don't. So why don't we do something like this? Why don't we put a quote 'clause' in your contract now and it will allow Turner to quote 'steal' you, and that way you'll earn a lot more money than you're earning now and you'll be a lot happier.'"

"You knew you were doing something that's a big no-no, and you're going to be hated."

—Shawn Michaels

"Bret thought it was a really good idea and so did Eric Bischoff and that group, so they paid Bret a lot more money than what I was paying for him, which I thought was a ridiculous deal to begin with for us. So, we allowed Bret to be stolen. Then from there, Bret refused at the time to, as we call it, do the honors—pass the championship on to someone else. It became problematic and I decided, 'Well, it's live television; here's what I'm going to do.' So there was a situation where I set up, what we call, a false finish."

To accomplish the plan, the infamous match between rivals Shawn Michaels and Bret Hart was talked through earlier in the day, with a spot planned for Michaels to lock Hart in Bret's own Sharpshooter submission hold.

Hart thought he was going to escape and the match would continue, but Michaels and referee Earl Hebner were in on the fix with McMahon. Hebner called for the bell once the hold was applied, making it appear that Hart had just tapped out to his own move right there in his home country of Canada.

"You knew you were doing something that's a big no-no, and you're going to be hated," says Michaels. "You don't know that it's going to last forever. I mean forever is a long time, you know? I wasn't sure that I was going to talk about it in every interview I ever did for the rest of my life. So, you know, you're going to be unpopular; it's not going to be fun. But at the end of the day, I do know what I was a part of and that was: it's going to go down; it's going to happen. It's like, ugh, that is so going to suck being that guy. It does. It happens, it's huge, it's everything—the nightmare that you imagine it could be it is, and then some. There was nothing appealing about it. I can remember going to do TV the next day, and, oh my goodness, I might get beat up. You don't know how the talent feels about it. You don't know how the producers feel about it. You don't know who knows about it and who doesn't."

"What I wanted that night was for Bret Hart not to leave the arena in Montreal as the WWE Champion. That's what I wanted, and that's what I got."

—Vince McMahon

"I've always told people I was only concerned about one guy, and that was Taker," continues Michaels. "I knew if he was cool with it or understood what went down, then that was really all that mattered to me. So I went to TV the next day, and he was in the office with Vince. And to this day I don't know what was said. I just know he came out, shook my hand, said we're cool and that was that."

"Shawn is a great soldier and will do anything for the sake of the business," says McMahon, "and as a matter of mutual respect, if I ask Shawn to do something, he, sometimes begrudgingly, would go do it. Shawn was a part of what I wanted in that night, and I simply wanted what was the right thing for the business. I know Bret Hart and I to this day disagree on what was right for the business, and certainly Bret is entitled to his opinion and I'm entitled to mine and everyone else is entitled to an opinion as well. But Shawn was a part of what I wanted that night. What I wanted that night was for Bret Hart not to leave the arena in Montreal as the WWE Champion. That's what I wanted, and that's what I got."

"You never know in life and in business the ramifications of something that you're involved with," says McMahon. "And when something does happen, you have to be flexible enough to deal with the reaction if in fact you're part of the action. This incident with Bret Hart just turned over a whole new leaf for our business in terms of creating the character Mr. McMahon. We were off to the races. So it's action/reaction. You have to be flexible; you have to read the tea leaves; you have to listen to the audience more than anything else. And the WWE audience was yelling bullshit at Mr. McMahon for what had happened. They took it out on me because they couldn't take it out on anyone else. So OK—how do I deal with that now? I know; I'll be who they want me to be."

VINCE TRANSFORMS INTO MR. MCMAHON

During the Attitude Era, Vince McMahon soaked up the boos more than any other talent, thanks to his actions in Montreal. And the WWE owner loved every minute.

"That's what the audience wanted; they wanted to boo me," says McMahon. "They wanted to boo me as a character because I had done Bret wrong. There was this huge swell, you know, and so why not take advantage of that? Give them what they want; let them boo me. It worked out really well in terms of how we adapted. And again, that's one of the things you have to be in life as well as in business—you have to be able to be flexible and adapt to what the audience wants. So if they want me to be a heel, then let's make something of it. I'll be a heel. And I knew that with Bret going down to WCW, he'd be no different than anyone else. There is professional jealousy and things of that nature. Bret had a big contract, and no one was getting along and it was going to be a mess. So I knew Bret was going to get his money, but it was going to be a mess. And that didn't work out well for Bret unfortunately. But it's listening to the audience, giving them what they want, being flexible, and having some degree of street smarts to know how to play that. It wound up a really good thing for us."

> **"This incident with Bret Hart just turned over a whole new leaf for our business in terms of creating the character Mr. McMahon. We were off to the races."**
>
> —Vince McMahon

Main image: Bret Hart looks for Vince McMahon backstage.
Inset: McMahon's infamous "Bret Screwed Bret" interview.

As for Hart, the Hit Man breaks down his side of the (still!) hotly debated story.

"People always say that Vince didn't have any choice, but it's totally not true," says Hart. "According to my contract back then, I had to wrestle 280 days a year for Vince McMahon. By the time I wrestled Shawn at *Survivor Series* that year where they screwed me out of the title, I had already worked something like 310 shows. I didn't even need to be there. I could've just told Vince that I already did my dates according to my contract. I could've told him to just take his championship and shove it and walk out. But I was a professional and I was giving him everything I could. I really didn't even have a problem losing the WWE Championship, but Shawn didn't have any respect for me and I didn't have any respect for him."

The mistrust even boiled over into real-life violence after the match. Hart first air-wrote the initials "WCW" for the fans, and then he went backstage and punched Vince McMahon.

"It was an uppercut and it was a little bit like that Buster Douglas punch on Mike Tyson," says Hart. "Maybe a little better than that if you can believe it."

WAS IT A WORK?

One of the interesting debates about Montreal is whether the entire episode was a legit screwjob or if Bret was in on the plot as a way to drum up attention and create the Mr. McMahon character. Kevin Nash shares his opinion: "To this day, I still have to raise a Rock eyebrow on it. When I watched it back, and they show the clip of Vince after he got socked, disheveled—knowing Vince at that time—I don't know. It just had that little bit of taste of work to it. Because I look at it and I say, 'Vince is the kind of guy that if he painted something in his house and he ran out of paint, and he had to go and get more, he would take a shower, get a manicure, put on a brand new suit, go buy the paint, come back, and switch out.' There was no way Vince would sell anything. Vince didn't sell the neck, the government. Vince no-sold the world. And for some reason, Vince let the world see him sell. And I just went, 'Work.' That's just my opinion. It still is. I'm allowed to have that. I don't believe the Warren Commission either, so I'm a conspiracy theory kind of guy." To Nash's way of thinking, Vince McMahon would never let on to anything bothering him, be it a broken neck or a federal trial. Yet for some reason, he took a punch from Bret and "sold" that he was hurt, which was completely out of character for him. For this reason, Nash believes Bret was in on it the whole time.

BROTHERS OF DESTRUCTION

It was May 1997 when Paul Bearer first let the world in on his bombshell secret. The devious manager not only had a new client, but that client was none other than Undertaker's half-brother Kane, a sibling Taker thought had died years ago when the family's funeral parlor went up in flames. Undertaker later admitted to starting the fire after initially blaming Kane.

Crazy as the origin story sounds, there's no denying the big-money results. The Kane/Undertaker saga led to some of the hardest-hitting encounters in WWE history, elevating both characters throughout the fiery narrative.

"With the Attitude Era, *Raw* went from being a wrestling show to being a cutting edge television show, and the Brothers of Destruction storyline really helped add a fantastic element to that," says Glenn Jacobs, the man behind Kane's mask. "The Kane/Undertaker story was almost like something out of Greek mythology. You have two brothers who are larger than life characters with super powers, and their whole reason for existence is to destroy one another or anybody who stands in their path."

KANE VS. UNDERTAKER: A LOOK BACK

WrestleMania XIV: Undertaker needs an unprecedented three Tombstones to defeat Kane.

Unforgiven 1998, Inferno Match: Undertaker defeats Kane in what is billed as "The Most Dangerous match in WWE history" by setting his brother's arm on fire.

WrestleMania XX: The Deadman returns after being buried alive by Kane and Mr McMahon at *Survivor Series* to defeat his brother.

Judgment Day 1998: Undertaker unleashes a fierce arsenal on Kane, but special referee Stone Cold Steve Austin then hits Taker with a Stone Cold Stunner, causing a no-contest.

Survivor Series 1998: Paul Bearer holds Kane's legs down to enable Undertaker to score the pinfall victory.

Inferno Match 2: Mr. McMahon orders an Inferno Match on *Raw* during the February 22, 1999 telecast. Once again, Undertaker wins, this time setting Kane's foot on fire.

SummerSlam 2000: Undertaker rips off Kane's mask.

Night of Champions 2010: Kane defeats Undertaker in a no-holds barred battle.

Hell in a Cell 2010: Kane beats his brother to retain the World Heavyweight Championship inside the Hell in a Cell structure that started it all.

While Bearer dropped hints about the sinister brother looking for revenge on screen, behind the scenes Jacobs was being introduced not only to Kane's character but to the heel's signature red look.

"I remember seeing pictures of Kane and the proposed outfit, and it wasn't anything that I envisioned," remembers Jacobs. "I envisioned Kane as this raving lunatic who escaped from a mental asylum or something like that. But when I saw the pictures, it looked more like a superhero costume. So I talked to Vince about it and expressed my concerns, but as he often does, he said, 'Trust me, it's going to be great.' I remember we had a meeting and Jim Ross was there, along with some of the talent relations people and some of the writing team. When they were talking about Kane, Vince said the optimal word about the costume: that it was 'cool.' It wasn't lunatic, it was cool. And that took Kane in a different direction than I would've thought. They did something completely different, and it was more of a superhero or super villain type of outfit. Then you add in all the bells and whistles with the pyro, and the fact that Undertaker was willing to work so hard to help me, and that says volumes in itself. I knew I could make it work if given the right opportunity. With the company behind it, the machine behind it, and Undertaker behind it, Kane became a can't-miss proposition."

This can't-miss proposition just so happened to debut during the main event of the *In Your House: Badd Blood* pay-per-view, headlined by the first ever Hell in a Cell match between Shawn Michaels and Undertaker.

Preliminary costume study for the Kane character.

> ## "With the company behind it, the machine behind it, and Undertaker behind it, Kane became a can't-miss proposition."
> —Glenn Jacobs

Says Jacobs: "It was arguably the best debut ever. I wasn't even in the match-up. It was Shawn Michaels versus Undertaker in their first match of consequence. Here you have the main event of a pay-per-view, and Hell in a Cell was this brand new concept, this brand new match. All I was thinking to myself was, 'I hope I don't mess this up.' And then to cost Undertaker the match by using his own move against him, especially at that point in time, when Undertaker was at the height of his career, I don't think they could have made my debut any better.

"I remember when I first came out toward the ring. It was super cool. You hear the music and you see this guy coming out with the pyrotechnic effects. On TV you have Vince McMahon screaming, 'It's gotta be Kane!' In the arena, the crowd wasn't sure what to think at first, but then they really got with it. We had this build up for months with Paul Bearer talking about Kane, and before that, you had this long history with Paul Bearer and Undertaker. The Kane story wasn't just terrific; it was one of the best stories WWE has ever told, because they planted the seeds then they let it die before the match with Undertaker and Shawn. So then the night became about the match, but then there's Kane; there's your payoff to the story, and we were just getting started."

UNDERTAKER KEEPS ROLLIN'

When the Attitude Era began, Undertaker was still playing the part first made famous during the more cartoon-like New Generation Era, in which he was known for battling the likes of King Mabel, Yokozuna, and Diesel. But in 1999, 'Taker introduced the world to a more evil, dark priest version of his persona. He added elements of Satanism and created his own stable known as The Ministry of Darkness. Not only did the Ministry perform Superstar sacrifices, they even orchestrated a kidnapping of Stephanie McMahon. In 2000, Undertaker saw an even more drastic change, ditching his funeral parlor persona altogether in favor of a biker character dubbed The American Badass, complete with Limp Bizkit and Kid Rock theme songs. In 2001, Undertaker debuted yet another look, calling himself "Big Evil" before capturing the WWE Hardcore title. The legendary Dead Man finally made his WWE return in 2004 to battle Kane at *WrestleMania XX*.

KANE TALKS KATIE VICK

"That was pushing the boundaries way too far. I think they thought it was going to be cutting edge at the time, but that just completely backfired. That was one of those things that I'd really like to forget. It just didn't work. It wasn't my idea in any capacity, and it just didn't come across like they thought it would. As good as some of the stuff was, this really wasn't good. In our attempt to be very cutting edge, sometimes things just don't work out."

After *Badd Blood*, Undertaker refused to fight his brother. But once Kane cost Taker the WWE Championship at the *Royal Rumble*, locking The Dead Man in a casket and then lighting it on fire, Undertaker had no choice but to escape the flames and challenge Kane to a match at *WrestleMania XIV*. Undertaker won the battle at *WrestleMania*, but Kane and Paul Bearer were determined to win the war. They attacked Taker after the match, and then set up WWE's first ever Inferno Match, playing off the duo's history with fire.

"Anytime you can introduce a new match in WWE, you know you're on to something special. This was a new concept built around the Kane character," says Jacobs, who counts his Inferno Match as one of the personal favorites of his career. "The match was limiting because of the fire, but it was also so unique and had such great visuals. It was a really special night."

BROTHERS OF DESTRUCTION: FIVE MATCHES TO WATCH

February 1, 2001
SmackDown
Undertaker and Kane vs. Rikishi and Haku
First Blood Match: Steel chairs, stairs, and even the announcers' table come into play in this brutal encounter that left both Islanders a bloody mess.

February 25, 2001
No Way Out 2001
Undertaker and Kane vs. The Dudley Boyz and Edge and Christian
Tables Match: It's six-man carnage, as all three teams lay waste to each other, both inside and out of the ring. After interference from Rikishi and Haku, The Dudley Boyz get the win—they 3-D Christian through a table.

April 29, 2001
Backlash 2001
Undertaker and Kane vs. Triple H and Stone Cold Steve Austin
After interference from Stephanie and Vince McMahon, The Two Man Power Trip capture the win—and the tag titles—after Triple H smashes Kane with his patented sledgehammer.

April 19, 2001
SmackDown
Undertaker and Kane vs. Edge and Christian
After Stone Cold Steve Austin and Triple H interfere to take down Kane, Undertaker ducks under a ConChairto, and then delivers a Last Ride to Christian for the victory. This is the first time the Brothers of Destruction win tag team gold.

November 3, 2006
SmackDown
Undertaker and Kane vs. Kennedy and MVP
After years of fighting, it was finally time for the Brothers of Destruction to reunite and once again do what they do best: wreak havoc. The brothers teamed to defeat Kennedy and MVP three times in one night. They finished off the heels with a double choke slam, followed by a Tombstone to Mr. Kennedy.

"They started calling our tag team The Brothers of Destruction, and really, how is anyone going to fight off two of the most powerful characters in WWE history?"

—Glenn Jacobs

UNDERTAKER TALKS ATTITUDE ERA

"It was a blast. We were living like rock stars. It really was tremendous. You have to realize that we're on the road over 250 dates a year. It wears you out, you know, it does. But when you go into an arena and it's standing room only, no tickets available, and the energy that those people are giving … And in going anywhere—anywhere you went you were recognized, you know? Rumor had it back then that I led a pretty rough nightlife, but … we didn't wait in lines, and you were treated well wherever you were at. I mean everybody wanted to be a part of it."

A few months later, the brothers reunited with Undertaker helping Kane defeat Stone Cold Steve Austin in a First Blood Match at *King of the Ring*. However, the brotherly love didn't last long as Undertaker turned on Kane at Judgment Day. He rejoined Paul Bearer, betraying his blood and turning heel, helping Kane become a fan favorite in the process.

"It was a little soap opera of who can you trust," says Jacobs. "Paul Bearer was the bridge between Undertaker and Kane, and Paul was very important in that. He turns his back on me, he returns to me, he turns his back on Taker … it was great stuff. Paul was as an important part of the package as any of us were."

Unfortunately for Kane, when he tried to take his own form of revenge during Undertaker's Buried Alive match against Austin during the *Rock Bottom* pay-per-view, The Corporation had Kane committed to an insane asylum. They released the Big Red Machine only after he agreed to join them.

Although Corporate Kane had a limited run, the back and forth between Kane and his brother continued throughout the years. At *SummerSlam* 2000, the two once again battled, with the brutal brawl culminating in Kane's unmasking at the hands of his brother.

"Eventually, we get back together and join forces," says Jacobs. "They started calling our tag team The Brothers of Destruction, and really, how is anyone going to fight off two of the most powerful characters in WWE history? It was great to work as a tag team, because with Kane and Undertaker, you had this compelling storyline told over a number of years. The fans were really into it, so it was fun to get a chance to be an official team for a while. To be able to tell these stories and get the reactions we wanted from the fans throughout the years, that's what this business is all about. That's what makes this business so rewarding."

As for Kane and Undertaker's relationship backstage, Jacobs says it has never been stronger. "The thing about Taker is, everything you ever hear about him backstage and how he's very professional and how hard he works at helping people is true. He's my role model. He's who I try to pattern myself after. You go out every night and you try to do the best that you can, no matter how many people may or may not be there. It doesn't matter how many people are watching, because those people bought tickets and they deserve the best that you can give them that particular night. So he's been my mentor, he's been my friend, and he's really been the guy who taught me more about being a businessman and an entertainer than anybody else."

"The thing about Taker is, everything you ever hear about him backstage and how he's very professional and how hard he works at helping people is true. He's my role model."

—Glenn Jacobs

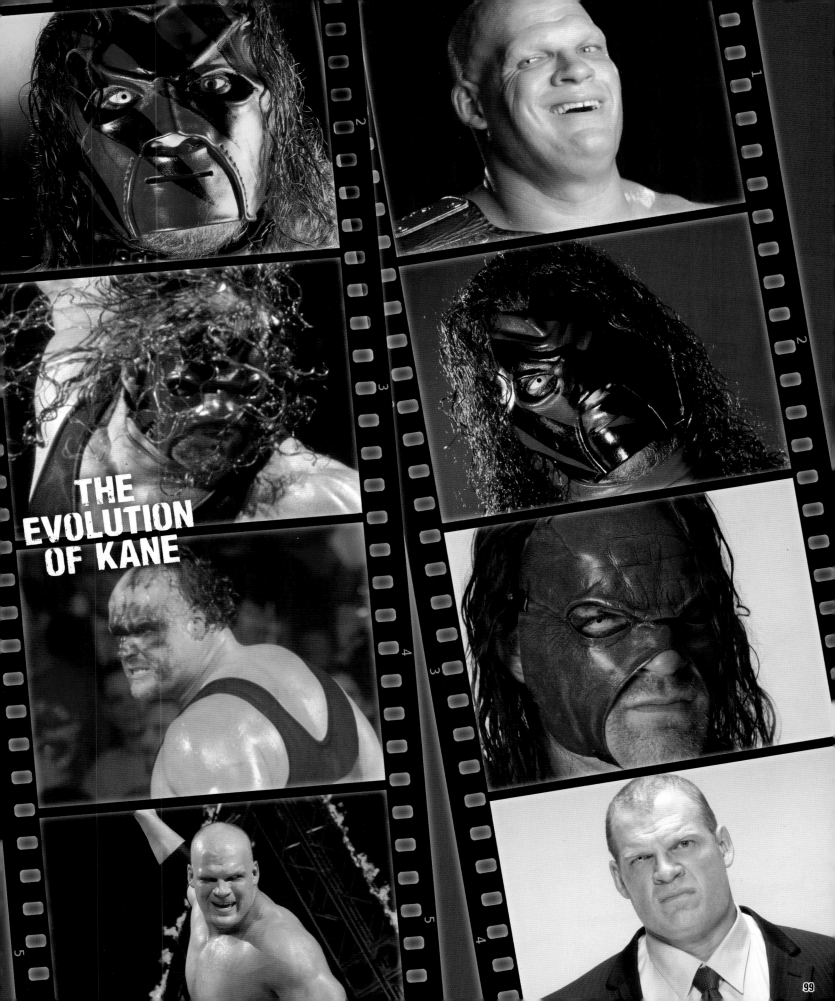

THE EVOLUTION OF KANE

CELEBRITIES

While celebrities from Lawrence Taylor to Muhammad Ali had appeared on various WWE shows throughout its past, it's safe to say that no athlete made more of a difference or drew more mainstream attention than Mike Tyson's appearance during the Attitude Era.

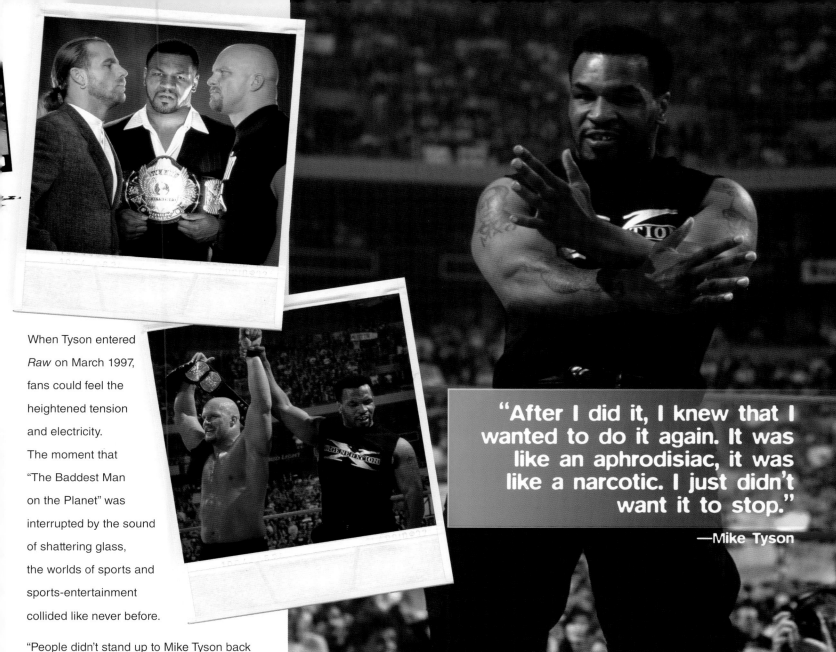

"After I did it, I knew that I wanted to do it again. It was like an aphrodisiac, it was like a narcotic. I just didn't want it to stop."

—Mike Tyson

When Tyson entered *Raw* on March 1997, fans could feel the heightened tension and electricity. The moment that "The Baddest Man on the Planet" was interrupted by the sound of shattering glass, the worlds of sports and sports-entertainment collided like never before.

"People didn't stand up to Mike Tyson back then, and when they did they got knocked out," says Shawn Michaels, who helped recruit Tyson to DX in the weeks headed to *WrestleMania XIV*.

"I remember the push-push, and I remember sitting there, thinking, 'Oh my gosh, Tyson's going to fight Austin, and this is going to be awesome," remembers Daniel Bryan. "Austin was everything you wanted in a WWE Superstar, and Tyson was 'The Baddest Man on the Planet' and crazy. So, when you heard they were actually going to fight, you thought, 'Oh my God, this is going to be wicked cool.'"

Says Jim Ross, "Mike Tyson's public image fit DX's identity to a T. Nobody wanted to touch Tyson because he was trouble. Problematic. Bad track record, PR nightmare, so what do you do? Well, you come to WWE and you just be yourself. So, Tyson came to WWE and aligned himself with DX."

Luckily for Stone Cold Steve Austin, the Tyson/DX partnership didn't last. Tyson not only counted the 1-2-3 to award Stone Cold the WWE Championship, but he even measured Michaels with a signature right hook to close out *WrestleMania*.

Adds Tyson, "When I walked out to the *WrestleMania* crowd in Boston, I had never experienced anything like that. And you have to understand, at that time, I was suspended in boxing, and man, that was just a really lifesaving experience financially. It was just something that I will never forget. It's just amazing. After I did it, I knew that I wanted to do it again. It was like an aphrodisiac, it was like a narcotic. I just didn't want it to stop."

"Pete Rose is great. If he hadn't been a baseball player, he would've made a great WWE Superstar."

—Kane

KANE TALKS PETE ROSE

"Pete Rose is great. If he hadn't been a baseball player, he would've made a great WWE Superstar. He was just all about entertainment, and he was one of those guys that, if you asked him to do something, he would do it. I'll never forget, he goes out there during *WrestleMania XIV* and does the best heel promo I've ever heard. 'I left Billy Buckner tickets at the box office, but he couldn't bend over and pick them up.' I've worked with Pete on a lot of stuff now, and I can't speak of him highly enough as an entertainer. I still remember *WrestleMania XX*, Pete Rose comes out to hit me with a baseball bat, but Rikishi takes the bat from him and poor Pete ends up taking the Stink Face. Pete signed that bat and gave it to me, so that was pretty awesome. We even had this one pay-per-view where kids were trick-or-treating for Halloween, and Pete was playing the grumpy old man until Kane showed up to scare him again. It's hilarious how many times our paths have crossed."

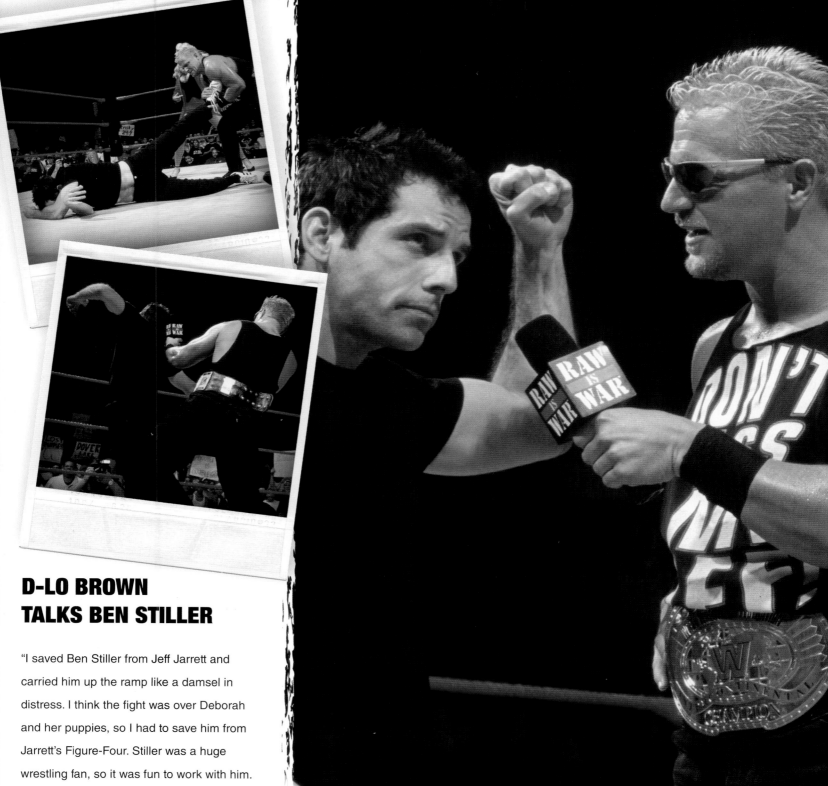

D-LO BROWN
TALKS BEN STILLER

"I saved Ben Stiller from Jeff Jarrett and carried him up the ramp like a damsel in distress. I think the fight was over Deborah and her puppies, so I had to save him from Jarrett's Figure-Four. Stiller was a huge wrestling fan, so it was fun to work with him. It's funny, because when wrestling is good, all of these closeted fans will come out of the woodwork and want to jump into the ring. When wrestling is going good, everyone wants to be involved, and Stiller was one of those guys who grew up a fan and always wanted a chance to be involved somehow."

"It's funny, because when wrestling is good, all of these closeted fans will come out of the woodwork and want to jump into the ring."

—D-Lo Brown

ROAD DOGG ON ARNOLD SCHWARZENEGGER PUNCHING TRIPLE H

"It was awesome to see a celebrity like Schwarzenegger willing to put himself out there because, especially in the movie business, they are so handled and so scripted. So when they let themselves go and open the door a little bit, it's really cool. But from what I understand, Hunter could have used a stuntman, because [laughs] I don't think Arnold knows his own strength.

CHRIS JERICHO ON WCW CELEBRITIES

"I think what happened was, when Vince brought in Mike Tyson, I think that Eric originally wanted to bring in Mike Tyson. Vince won and it's just that: 'We've gotta bring in some more celebrities.' And at first it was cool. I mean, the first Rodman, Malone match was kind of a cool idea. Rodman was a jerk, Karl Malone was very cool. Rodman fell asleep at ringside because they had been drinking all night long and showed up, I think, at seven o'clock for the taping that started at 7:30. Fine, they paid him his three and a half million, he didn't take any of it seriously and split. Fine. I thought that the Jay Leno thing was getting ridiculous, because it might've gotten some promotion and some press, but on the backhand it totally sold out the business. It totally castrated the business 'cause here's Jay Leno beating up Hulk Hogan. And I remember seeing the first move was Hogan getting put in an armbar by Jay Leno, and they sat there for about a minute, and I was like, 'Why, what are they doing?' Meanwhile, all the photographers are taking pictures. Of course, the next day front cover, here's Hogan in an armbar with Jay Leno. Hogan was very smart—he got his. That's when it started getting ridiculous. Then Megadeth is playing, then they get the Kiss guy, then David Arquette's the World Champion. It's like, nobody cared about any of these people—they cared about Karl Malone and Dennis Rodman 'cause it was the first time they'd ever seen that. The Jay Leno thing, the people thought was a joke, and it was. I mean, here you have a 50-year-old, out-of-shape man working against Hulk Hogan. It just—there's a disconnect and it was a gimmick. They did what they did but it was another reason. … Master P, the No-Limit Soldiers, what a total bomb that was. But they didn't ever really learn."

D-GENERATION X

"I was half naked on TV. We were playing strip poker on TV, I'm scratching my, you know, Johnson."
—Shawn Michaels

When *WCW Nitro* first launched and *Raw* was getting destroyed in the ratings, Shawn Michaels and Triple H had an idea that helped light a fire under the entire company: D-Generation X.

"Let us loose," Michaels remembers telling Vince McMahon, wanting the company to ditch the cartoon-like characters of Doink the Clown and The Goon in favor of edgier content, including crotch chops, a "suck it" catch phrase, and a penis-joke-to-headlock ratio that was almost unthinkable until they did it live on *Raw*, of course. "Finally, he [Vince] just had enough, like whatever the classy, high road he had convinced himself we were doing wasn't working.

"We just went out there, and Hunter and I we just said everything under the sun … and we still got in trouble. 'You can't say that!' I don't know. I was half naked on TV. We were playing strip poker on TV, I'm scratching my, you know, Johnson. I'm wearing a pair of boxers out there. I mean, I'm getting hammered on TV. I'm out there, people think, 'let's have him playing strip poker and stuff like that.' And it's Shawn pretending to be drinking Jack, but it will be tea. [Shakes head] I was at a different place in my life. I did the old switcheroo. I'm drinking Jack Daniels on TV, just getting lit."

And the crowd ate up every minute, even if the television execs at USA didn't necessarily agree. "USA network finally sends us this letter to Vince," remembers Michaels. "He [Vince] reads us what they are saying, and Hunter and I are like, whatever, 'Sorry, sorry, sorry.'"

But after McMahon leaves the room, *Raw* creative writer Vince Russo has an idea. He wants to setup a faux apology on *Raw* where Michaels and Triple H read the letter on air, saying all the words they're being told not to say, except with beeps over anything objectionable. "And man, we go out there and do this thing, and we read their letter," says Michaels. "'USA network standards and practices, you cannot say the word *beep*.' We are just going through this litany of curse words, and 'we can't make reference to our extremely enormous genitalia.'

"They are putting the censor up and stuff like that. And to this day, when I'm reading it and you see Hunter doing his best not to laugh. And finally I end up with the Bill Clinton 'I did not sleep with a young intern but …' it was just fun. It's just hilarious. Oh my goodness, and Vince goes ballistic." So ballistic, that Michaels and Triple H actually thought they were going to get fired. Instead, McMahon calls the two Superstars into his office.

"We went in and said, 'This is the one, we're going to get fired for sure,'" says Michaels. "We've pushed him too far. He goes, 'You won't believe this … that skit you did last week, the USA Network, they loved it! They thought it was hilarious!' And that was it. He told us right there, I'm cutting you loose." And we started doing the skits. We're doing the BBQ with the big sausages … more penis jokes than you can shake a stick at. More boob stuff. We were pushing every taboo on TV. The tide started to shift."

"He told us right there, 'I'm cutting you loose.' And we started doing the skits. We're doing the BBQ with the big sausages … more penis jokes than you can shake a stick at. More boob stuff."

—Shawn Michaels

Adds Triple H, "Steve said 'ass' and gave people the finger on TV, but we were dropping our drawers and telling people to suck it. We were bucking the system heavily, and we were not being embraced behind the scenes for what we were doing. Vince gave us the opportunity, but we were getting reamed every time we came back through the curtain. It was not popular with the producers or Vince. They just didn't get it."

But for fans who thought DX was just a copy of WCW's New World Order, Michaels couldn't disagree more. "We weren't doing that. We were doing sophomoric, low brow … we were making penis jokes," says Michaels. "We were silly and stupid; they were trying to be cool. We weren't trying to be cool. We just ended up being cool because we were so stupid."

"Sophomoric hijinks were hilarious. That's how we are in real life. One of us is still like that. He is; I'm a little less so. Practically a real person now. But I don't see the comparison. They didn't dress up in a lot of stuff. You know what I mean? They beat everybody up all the time, we got beat up all the time. We were just two guys acting like idiots."

Unfortunately for Michaels, an injury to his back meant an early exit from the sausage fest that he helped create. But that didn't mean it was time to end the increasingly popular faction, a faction many credit with helping start the Attitude Era. In fact, with Triple H becoming the new leader, things were just getting started.

March 30, 1998, a new DX is born with Road Dogg, Billy Gunn, and a returning X-Pac joining the crew. "I'll be honest. There's an argument that can be made that (the new) DX was better than mine and Hunter's," admits Michaels. "Now, they were in the full swing of stuff and the audience was growing. We were the foundation doing stuff, but they got to expand on all of that."

"We gained popularity because they gave us a live mic and let us do what we wanted to do," says Road Dogg. "But I remember when we were first approached about joining DX. Billy and I acted all cool and told them that we'd think about it, but when we walked around the corner, we were doing back flips. It was crazy. We were so excited to join. All the stars aligned and everything just felt right as we carried a camera around with us and acted our way through some crazy scenarios. We just free-styled everything and had fun. And having fun translated to the viewing audience. We had a good time; it just happened that they were filming when we did it."

The new DX continued to push the envelope with infamous skits mimicking and even dressing up as The Nation. And of course, possibly the most memorable scene in *Raw* history was when DX took an army tank and tried to invade a live episode of *WCW Nitro*.

"To tell you the truth, we had no idea what we were doing at all. We were totally winging it when we got to *Nitro*," says Road Dogg. "We would've loved to have actually gotten into the building. But if we made it in, who knows what would've happened. They probably would've beaten the fire out of us, but I know I had a couple of brothers on the inside who would've swung on my side.

"I don't know how far we would've taken it, but to be honest, I couldn't believe how far we took it in the first place," continues Road Dogg. "We got to TV that day, and they said, 'Hey, we're going to go invade WCW.' I thought it was the coolest thing I had ever heard. Next thing I knew, we're getting pulled over by the cops for driving a simulated tank down the road. We didn't have permits or anything. We were just trying to take things as far as we could. Hey, if we would've gotten into the building and we got beat up, that would've been great TV, too."

ROAD DOGG ON CHYNA'S CONTRIBUTION TO DX

"People don't realize how important Chyna was to the group. She has a really great sense of humor. So she and I and Hunter would constantly bounce ideas off each other on how we can raise the bar even further. Like, I'd say, 'Chyna, hit me in the balls with the rifle,' and I'd sell that and it would be funny. She was an intricate part to the funny stuff that we did. On camera, she was the big, tough girl, but behind the scenes she was really funny and really helped contribute to the overall tone of what DX was trying to accomplish. Nobody gives her credit for this aspect because of the simple fact that nobody outside the locker room even knew."

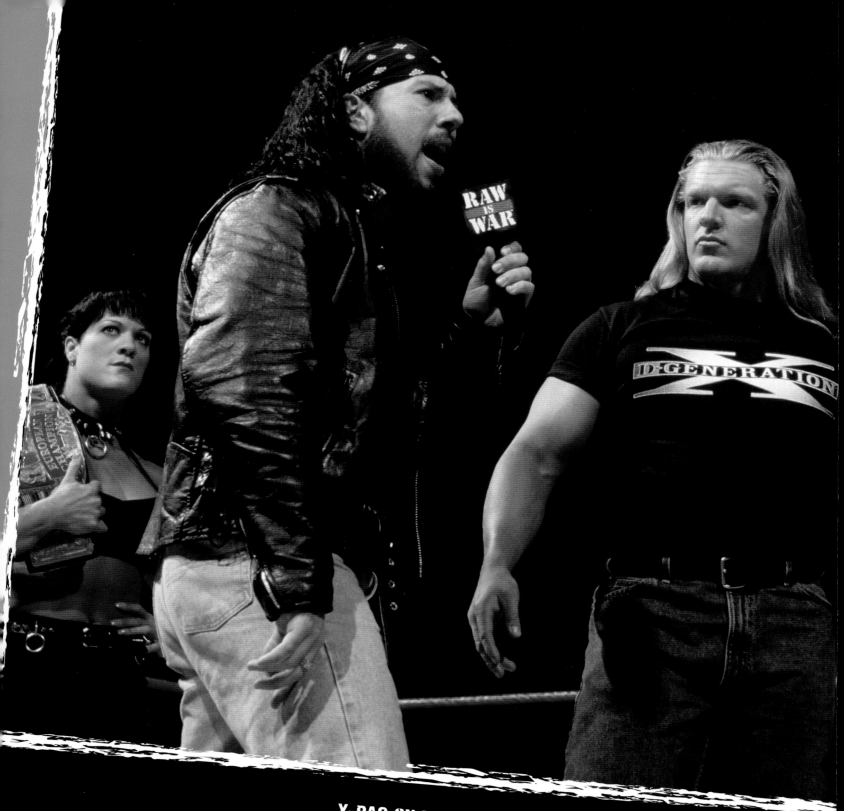

X-PAC ON HIS DX DEBUT

"People knew I was coming out that night. They were expecting to hear something, and thank God I think I delivered … The obligatory jab to Hogan and Bischoff—and I like the Hulk, I don't have any problems with Eric either. At the time I did, but you know, when somebody talks shit about you on national TV and you don't retort, you're a pussy. It's not like it was just some jabroni talking shit about me that you don't want to even give credence to; it's Hulk Hogan. And they were winning in the ratings at the time, barely. So, gee, it wasn't too long after that we started kicking their ass though, huh, coincidentally."

But even with their success on camera, behind the scenes the group wasn't always the easiest for the creative team to handle. "DX was challenging behind the scenes because you had guys who were very skilled bell to bell. Their skills could never be overrated; they were that good. They were also very outspoken in front of the camera. They would go off and create their own content, and sometimes it could step over the line, but they liked the ability to create their own content the best they could," says Jim Ross. "There wasn't a big difference in how they were behind the scenes and how they were in front of the camera. The best stars are the ones whose TV personas closely resemble their real selves. WWE Superstars are not known—unless you're Dwayne Johnson—for being great actors. They're known for being amplified and embellished versions of themselves. That's what the best Superstars are. They're the ones who can make their TV personas who they are multiplied times two.

"So when you have a group of wise cracking, defiant, edgy, entertaining guys like DX, if you saw them at catering, they were modified versions of exactly who you saw on TV," continues Ross. "When they had Shawn, Hunter, Billy Gunn, Road Dogg, and X-Pac, all of those guys were well versed in the business. None of them were neophytes. They were all experienced pros. Shawn Michaels is arguably the greatest in-ring performer ever. So that didn't hurt DX's launch. If you're going to launch a new basketball team, it's like having Michael Jordan in his prime. Then you have Triple H, who had a great vision and a great instinctual feel for the business way beyond his years. Even though his character on television showed off his intellect and his confidence in himself, he would know when to shut it down behind the scenes. He was always the man of reason in that DX group. The others would almost forget the camera wasn't rolling, and they'd still be acting defiant or be challenging to be around. But Paul Levesque was always the voice of reason. Road Dogg had been a Marine in the Persian Gulf and was from a wrestling family, and now he was getting his opportunity to live his dream. Billy Gunn's previous claim to fame was being part of the Smoking Gunns. Great team, but they never had the success DX had. Sean Waltman, who was X-Pac, was the youngest of the group, a lifelong fan who started wrestling as a teenager, making little to no money while paying his dues. He always had to overcome the label that he was too small to be a star. So you had an interesting, combustible group of personalities."

"We got to TV that day, and they said, 'Hey, we're going to go invade WCW.' I thought it was the coolest thing I had ever heard."

—Road Dogg

"Rude didn't hang out with us. He was his own entity. I don't even know who or why they wanted to put him in there. We just went, 'cool, that's fine.' We had Chyna in there. I honestly couldn't say. We weren't surprised when Rude jumped ship in the middle of the night. You know, it's funny because it's like, '[gasp] He's going to be on both shows, because our show is taped and, word is, he's going to show up live on their show tonight.' Of course everyone's like, 'What's that going to do?' And me and Hunter are like, 'Pfft, who cares?' Nothing you could do about it. He wasn't the foundation of DX. That's why guys could leave. There only needed to be two guys there the whole time; that's me and Hunter, and that was never gonna change."

"He wasn't the foundation of DX. That's why guys could leave. There only needed to be two guys there the whole time; that's me and Hunter, and that was never gonna change."

—Shawn Michaels

LEMEN BOYS AND GIRLS CHILDRE
PROUDLY BRINGS TO YOU IT'S WW
E ROAD DAWG JESSE JAMES THE
S*CK
DOWN HERE!
HEY CAMERAMAN 2 WORDS S*CK IT
JIM SUCK DX!

OF ALL AGES

TAG TEAM CHAMPIONS

D ASS BILLY GUNN

E GOT TWO WORLDS FOR

S·U·C·K·IT

> "I'll be honest. There's an argument that can be made that (the new) DX was better than mine and Hunter's."
>
> —Shawn Michaels

Ross continues, "They were a huge, huge part of the Attitude Era. The Era worked because it wasn't a one-trick pony. Vince McMahon couldn't be on the road for all the live events. So, he could only be a part-time villain on television because he had to go back to the boardroom during the week and run the business end of the company. We had to have depth. DX was one of those groups that not only provided depth, but they went out and tried to steal the show night after night."

Adds Vince McMahon: "I was always entertained, personally speaking, with everything that they did. Professionally I thought that maybe, yeah, we would get a few phone calls, letters. … DX crossed a lot of lines and, to their credit, they did because I listened to them and more specifically listened to the audience's reaction to them. The audience was loving DX, so I was going to love DX.

"DX was revolutionary, so much fun, and a breath of fresh air in the business. At the same time, wow, you walk the edge so many times in this business and in life—if you're living life—and DX was right on the edge. Sometimes a little bit over, sometimes not, but they were right on the edge in everything they were doing. And we never experienced a DX before with the 'suck it' chants, the gestures, and some of the things that they did with Chyna, X-Pac, Triple H and Shawn, the original DX. I mean highly entertaining, off-the-chart entertaining. And I think that's why the public accepted them, because they were doing these outlandish kinds of things. But yet they were almost winking at you, sometimes they were, hmm, out of line. But nonetheless you were always entertained."

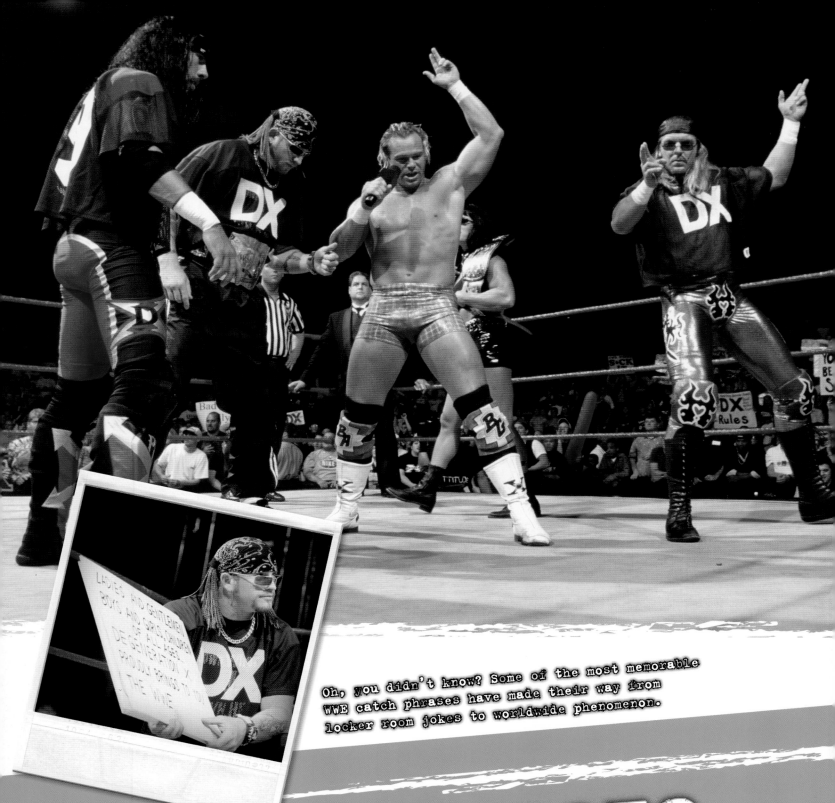

Oh, you didn't know? Some of the most memorable WWE catch phrases have made their way from locker room jokes to worldwide phenomenon.

CATCH PHRASES

Says Road Dogg, "I used to always say, 'Oh you didn't know? You better call somebody,' just playing around backstage. There used be this guy, The Underfaker. He was the fake Undertaker for a while, and then he wrestled in DOA as Chainz. Me and him were old friends, and we used to always change it up, like 'You better page somebody,' or 'You better fax somebody.' So I told him one night, I said, 'Hey, I'm going to say this tonight.' But he didn't believe me. So I went out there for our live event and I did it just for him. He got such a kick out of it, and then so many other people got a kick out of it, that a joke I did just to make people laugh backstage ended up really catching on with the fans.

"I just always thought about the ringmaster at the circus. He goes out there with the mic and he drums up business and acts like a hype man for the team. Then, once the 'Oh, you didn't know' got over, the rest was me just talking on the way to the ring. They told me, 'Take a microphone down to the ring and say whatever you want.' So a lot of what I was doing was just trying to make the other guys in DX laugh. I knew if I could make them laugh, it would entertain the crowd as well. This is the type of stuff you can't script. It's organic, it takes roots, and once the mob gets ahold of it and makes it their own, you have to keep going with it. The key to coming up with catch phrases is guys just messing around and being extensions of themselves."

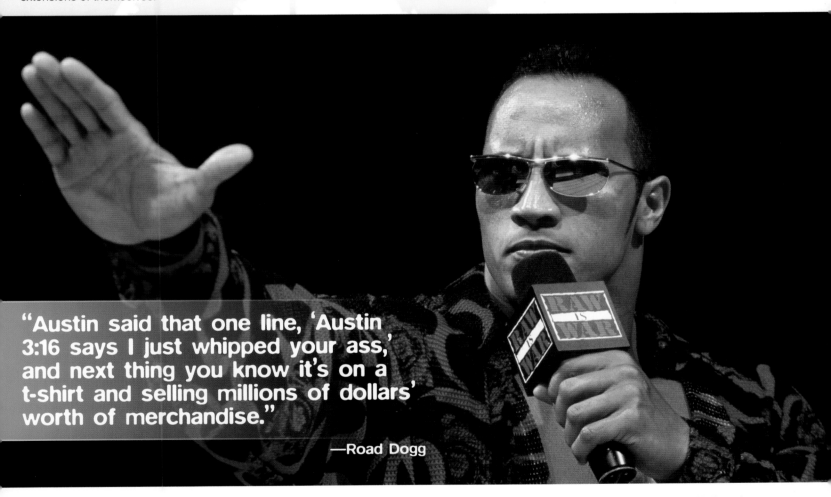

"Austin said that one line, 'Austin 3:16 says I just whipped your ass,' and next thing you know it's on a t-shirt and selling millions of dollars' worth of merchandise."

—Road Dogg

Ron Simmons agrees, revealing that The Rock's famous "Know your role" line was something Simmons used to say to his other Nation of Domination members behind the scenes. "I used to say 'know your role' all the time to the guys. Then one day, The Rock took it and used it on air, and it became one of his catchphrases. The Rock always had the athleticism, but when he came to The Nation, he would watch and listen to everything and everybody, tweaking sayings he might hear in a rap song or in the car ride on the way to the show. The next thing you knew, he was saying it on *Raw* and people were making signs with all these phrases. It was incredible to see."

Adds Road Dogg, "Austin said that one line, 'Austin 3:16 says I just whipped your ass,' and next thing you know it's on a t-shirt and selling millions of dollars' worth of merchandise. You just never know what society is going to latch onto."

TOP ATTITUDE ERA CATCH PHRASES

Stone Cold Steve Austin: "And that's the bottom line, cause Stone Cold said so."

Val Venis: "Hello, ladies."

The Rock: "It doesn't matter what your name is!"

Chris Jericho: "Welcome to Raw is Jericho."

Edge and Christian: "So, for the benefit of those with flash photography, we have a brand new pose just for you."

Vince McMahon: "You're fired!"

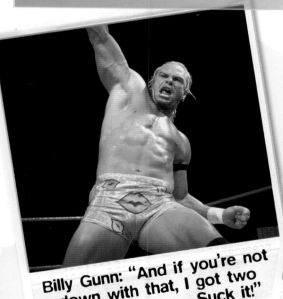

Billy Gunn: "And if you're not down with that, I got two words for you ... Suck it!"

Stone Cold Steve Austin: "Austin 3:16 says I just whipped your ass."

Road Dogg: "Oh, you didn't know!?! Your ass better call somebody."

Road Dogg: "Ladies and gentleman, boys and girls, children of all ages. D-Generation X proudly brings to you its WWE Tag Team Champions of the wooooorld! The Road Dogg Jesse James, the Badass, Billy Gunn ... the New Age Outlaws."

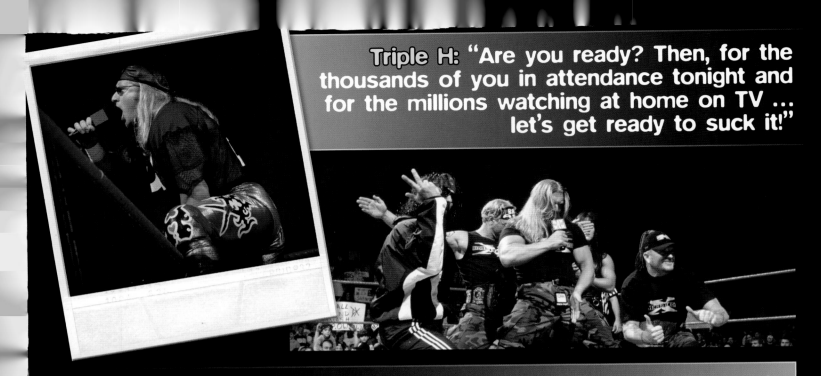

Triple H: "Are you ready? Then, for the thousands of you in attendance tonight and for the millions watching at home on TV ... let's get ready to suck it!"

The Rock: "It doesn't matter what you call it—Hell in a Cell, Rage in a Cage, Painus in Your Anus—the only thing that matters is that The Rock is going in there Sunday night to do what The Rock does best: layeth the smacketh down and get back The Rock's WWE title."

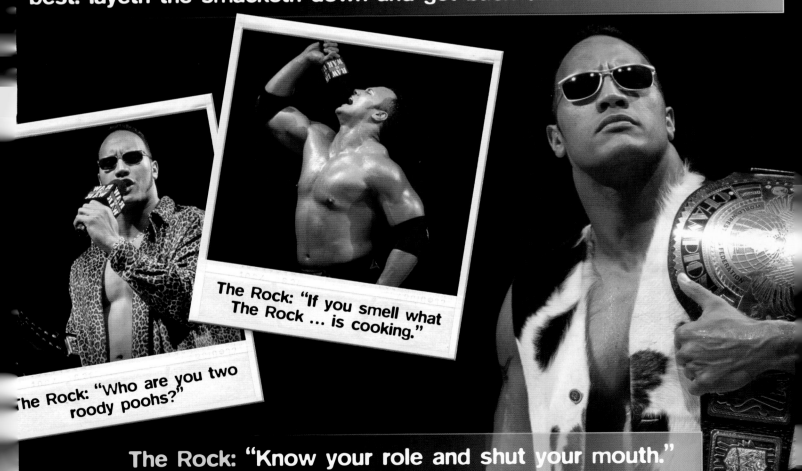

The Rock: "If you smell what The Rock ... is cooking."

The Rock: "Who are you two roody poohs?"

The Rock: "Know your role and shut your mouth."

Bubba Ray Dudley:
"D-Von, get the tables!"

The Godfather:
"It's time once again to get aboard the hooooooo train."

Kurt Angle:
"It's true, it's damn true."

Kurt Angle:
"Intensity. Integrity. Intelligence."

D-Lo Brown:
"You better recognize."

Trish Stratus:
"Stratusfaction guaranteed."

Cactus Jack:
"Bang! Bang!"

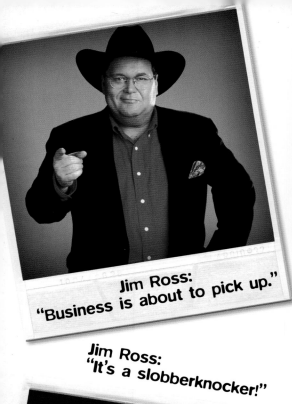

Jim Ross: "Business is about to pick up."

Jim Ross: "It's a slobberknocker!"

The Rock: "The Rock does smell what you're cooking. And quite frankly, Chris Jericho, what you're cooking smells like 100% grade-A, money back guaranteed, one big bucket of Canadian moose piss. You see, Chris Jericho, you come out here and run your mouth about how you tasted WWE gold. But the fact of the matter is that The Rock has lived WWE gold, and The Rock will be putting it down on anybody who stands in his way. So, whether it's you, Chris Jericho, Chris Jericho's daddy, Chris Jericho's mama, Uncle Joe Jericho with the glass eye, or maybe it's grandpa Jimmy-Jack Jericho with the iron lung … or hell, it might even be grandma Jezebel Jericho with the Double-X dirty panties. The only thing that matters, Chris Jericho, is that we have one big family reunion. You bring them all so The Rock can take his hand and layeth the smacketh down on all their candy asses."

Mankind: "Have a nice day!"

Chris Jericho: "I don't give a Brahma bull's ass what The Rock has to say. Just bring it? Bring what, a vomit bag? A Fig Newton? How about Y2J telling you to shut the hell up."

CLASSIC ROCK

"Finally, The Rock has come back to Las Vegas. Undertaker, Mankind, Kane, and Big Show. The Rock says all four of you jabronis can go down to the Tropicana hotel—it's right up the road. You find the absolute best slot machine you can find, and you can't miss it—it's got a big Brahma Bull on the front, and it says 'The People's Slot Machine.' And then, one of you jabronis can pull the handle, and there it is: one Brahma Bull, two Brahma Bulls, three Brahma Bulls. You jabronis hit the jackpot! And then, all of a sudden, you're jumping around like a bunch of idiots. Undertaker, with his Mickey Mouse tattoos and his 33-pound head, jumping around, screaming like a girl. Eeeehhhhh! Eeehhhh! Kane running around doing cartwheels and scaring everyone in the casino. 'I won, I won, let's party!' And the biggest goof of them all, The Big Slow, scaring all of The Rock's fans [raises his hands to mimic Big Show while screaming]. And then, the doors open and The Rock arrives. And as The Rock looks at all four of you jabronis, with tears rolling down your cheeks and piss rolling down your legs, The Rock says he's going to gather up all the gold coins you guys won. And in front of the millions (and millions!) of Rock's fans, he's going to shine all of the gold coins up … shine all the gold coins up, turn them sons of bitches sideways, and stick them straight up your candy ass."

KING OF KINGS

Hunter Hearst-Helmsley was supposed to be crowned *King of the Ring* in 1996. That's right. The Attitude Era as we know it—the Austin 3:16, the middle fingers, and the rise of the anti-hero—almost didn't happen.

If Triple H, a.k.a. WWE's EVP of Talent, Live Events and Creative Paul Levesque, had won *King of the Ring*, Stone Cold Steve Austin wouldn't have had the opportunity to ad-lib. He wouldn't have had the platform to talk trash. But thanks to an unforeseen, unscripted night in Madison Square Garden, the Stone Cold phenomenon was born.

"I was supposed to win *King of the Ring*. I was supposed to go from winning *King of the Ring* into a huge program with Shawn for the World Title," says Levesque. Instead, the Superstar found himself in a closed-door meeting with the WWE owner, where McMahon threatened to fire him over what is now dubbed "The Curtain Call." "Kevin's gone, Scott's gone, Kid wasn't there, and Shawn's champion. It doesn't take a genius to see that shit-ball rolling downhill," says Levesque. "I went from winning the *King of the Ring* to getting DDT'd in the first round and Jake sticking the snake down my pants, and getting beat by every guy here every week in every situation."

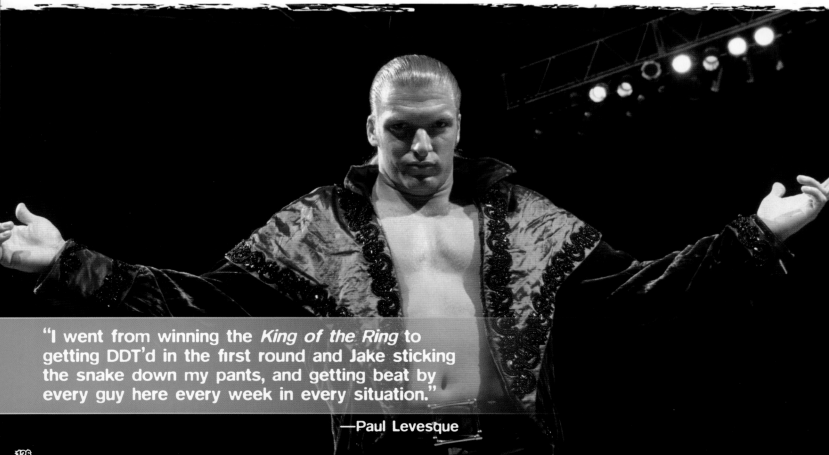

"I went from winning the *King of the Ring* to getting DDT'd in the first round and Jake sticking the snake down my pants, and getting beat by every guy here every week in every situation."

—Paul Levesque

Eventually, the losing streak came to an end, but not before Vince tried to give the Hunter Hearst-Helmsley character some heat by pairing him with Mr. Perfect, Curt Hennig. The problem? Hennig signed with WCW out of the blue, leaving Triple H without an enforcer. McMahon then pitched Levesque on teaming with The Honky Tonk Man. The idea was met with silence, frustrating McMahon even further.

"We were racking our brains trying to think of something different," says Levesque. "We came back from a show one night and we walked in the hotel and there's this jacked-up chick in the lobby. She walks over and she's like, 'I'm sorry, I just wanted to introduce myself.'" The jacked chick was Chyna, and that idea Levesque was looking for was now staring him in the face.

"Shawn and I started talking to her. I think both of us were like, 'Holy cow. This big giant jacked-up chic looks like she can kill people,'" laughs Levesque. "How much heat is that if I have a chick for a heater?"

Hunter Hearst Helmsley
2·24·96
Red/BLK. combo

"Hot"

Preliminary costume study for the Hunter Hearst-Helmsley character.

"The matches that I had with Triple H in 2000 and 2001 were probably the greatest matches I've ever had."

—The Rock

THE ROCK TALKS TRIPLE H RIVALRY

"The matches that I had with Triple H in 2000 and 2001 were probably the greatest matches I've ever had. And I mean that respectfully in terms of wrestling Hulk Hogan, Stone Cold Steve Austin, Mick Foley, even Undertaker. Triple H and myself had a very unique bond and very unique chemistry. At that time, we were hungry. Hungry, hungry, hungry to go out, and it didn't matter to us who was going to win, lose, or be WWE Champion. We didn't care. The only thing that mattered was that we would get on the road and we would work these live events or we would work *Raw* or the pay-per-views or *SmackDown*, and we just wanted to move and shake those cities."

SHAWN MICHAELS TALKS TRIPLE H

"The one thing about Hunter, he doesn't let a lot of people know what he's really like. He doesn't put a lot out there. But he's funny, he's sarcastic. In his own way, he wasn't quite the troublemaker; certainly wasn't what I was. I don't want to say that he's not nearly as obnoxious, because he is to his friends, he is to us, he is to me. But he's got a little bit more subtle approach to it. So when he first got here, he would put it out there and bring it back, put it out there and bring it back. Sounds like a fishing line—you throw it out farther each time. And then before you know it, he's as far off the farm as the rest of us, certainly from an attitude standpoint. I guess the thing is he didn't do all the extra-curricular stuff that we did, but he was always there, always had our back. And honestly, he could have left at any time. He saw that things were not progressively getting better as far as a popularity standpoint for us, but that never bothered him a bit."

"Then Chyna would pick up a 300-pound guy and slam him legit, and everybody would freak out ... It just took off."

—Paul Levesque

"When we pitched it to Vince, he thought we were out of our minds. He was like, 'No one's going to sell for a girl,' and he just hated it. We kept badgering him to try it. Then I got the *Rumble* that year. When I walked into the *Rumble*, I looked on the sheet for when my match was going to be on with Goldust and I see Curtis Hughes' name next to mine. And I'm like, 'Mr. Hughes—what?' Then I went to Vince and he said, 'Yeah, it's Curtis; he's going to be your bodyguard.' And I responded, 'No offense—I like Curtis—but, Vince, that's been done a million times.' So Curtis starts with me that night. A week later, we go to Madison Square Garden and Curtis Hughes' blood pressure is like 400 over 300 or something. He'd not bothered to get a physical and he was unhealthy as could be. They took him to the hospital and that was done."

"So back to the drawing board," continues Levesque. "We got to the point where we'd still be just badgering Vince. Somehow, in the meantime, Kevin Nash or somebody had thrown Chyna's name out to WCW and they were trying to hire her. So we were like, 'Vince, WCW is going to bring her in. Can we just do it?' Vince's response continued to be: 'It's not going to work. It's a terrible idea.' Then we got to Lowell, Massachusetts and it was the night Shawn lost his smile. I knew Shawn was handing over the title that night. I walked in and Vince called me downstairs to the office and said, 'I need you to drop the title to this new kid Rocky Maivia.' I was IC champ. Vince said, 'We just need something up on the show,' you know what I mean, like some positive. I was thinking: The kid they're chanting 'Die Rocky Die' for is going to be the positive? All right, that's cool with me. I was bummed out for Shawn and whatever; it was just a downer. I think Vince felt bad. He was trying to get me back on a roll, but things weren't panning out. Plus, he was asking me to drop the IC title. So Vince said, 'If you want, you can bring that chick in with you. Start her next month. But she's on you, and if she screws up it's your fault.'"

When Chyna debuted in Berlin, jumping over the barrier wall to interfere in his match, Levesque says some of the boys in the back were already grumbling about not wanting to sell for her.

"Then she would pick up a 300-pound guy and slam him legit, and everybody would freak out. And when the boys freak out, you realize: If they are freaking out, people are going to go crazy, and I want that reaction so she can slam me. It just took off. It was a great addition and it was a great spark. Shawn and I also had been badgering Vince about putting us together and we wanted to do this group. And that kind of was a beginning. It started to take off and things started to go."

The Triple H/Chyna pairing became one of the most memorable of the Attitude Era. The two teamed with Shawn Michaels to originate D-Generation X. Then, when HBK was injured, the duo helped lead a newer, even more outrageous version of the group, thanks to the additions of Road Dogg, Billy Gunn, and former Kliq member X-Pac.

It was at that point when fans first started to realize that Triple H was more than just Shawn Michaels' sidekick. In a series of memorable matches against The Rock, the two ambitious, cocky stars showed the WWE Universe where the main event scene was headed. And as Triple H continued to evolve his character from the smug aristocrat, to the smug degenerate, to the smug Cerebral Assassin now known as The Game, he continued to move up the card, especially after he decided to kidnap Stephanie McMahon from her wedding with Test and married her himself in a drive-through Vegas chapel.

The McMahon-Helmsley faction was born. Similar to the current-day Authority, the new group—assisted by DX members X-Pac, Road Dogg, and Billy Gunn—was all about power, especially after Triple H defeated Mankind (Mick Foley) to win his first WWE Championship.

"Mick, in a lot of ways, put me on the map," says Levesque. "Mick and I have talked about it a million times, but there were points in time where he wasn't a big star then, either, and we were both trying to prove ourselves. Together, we were doing things to go out there and steal the show." And the two did exactly that, delivering a pair of classic/vicious matches at *The Royal Rumble* and *No Way Out* in 2000.

Says Levesque, "Mick is one of those guys that, we had a great chemistry together and were really, really good for each other. I think he added a level of toughness to Triple H that was never there before that."

Triple H was rolling. Not only was he the first heel ever to win a main event match at *WrestleMania* (2000), but after his fierce fights against Foley, he became involved in one of the most memorable storylines of the era, a love triangle between himself, his onscreen (and future real world) wife Stephanie McMahon, and Olympic Gold Medalist Kurt Angle.

From there, rivalries with Austin and Undertaker helped solidify Triple H as one of the elite Superstars of his generation. Still, it makes one wonder how the industry would've changed if it indeed was Helmsley who won the *King of the Ring* and not Austin, or if Helmsley would've teamed with The Honky Tonk Man instead of Chyna. The entire fate of the WWE changed the night of The Curtain Call, and even Levesque will admit that it was a change for the better.

"I look at it now and I go, you know what, I wasn't ready," admits Levesque. "I wasn't ready to win *King of the Ring*. I wasn't ready to work with Shawn for the title. At the time, would it have been great? Yeah, it would've been an awesome experience. But looking back on it, I'm glad it didn't happen. You know it was the right time for Austin and Austin 3:16 and that whole shift and all those things. It wasn't the right time for me yet, but later it was. Everything happens for a reason and part of me is glad I went through all that. Like they say, what doesn't kill you makes you stronger, and this made me stronger, made me a better performer, made me a stronger business man, made me a stronger everything. I learned a lot from that."

"I look at it now and I go, you know what, I wasn't ready. I wasn't ready to win *King of the Ring*. I wasn't ready to work with Shawn for the title."

—Paul Levesque

TRIPLE H AND STEPHANIE

After an on-screen relationship between characters (and a kidnapping that led to a wedding) turned into a real-deal romance for Paul Levesque and Stephanie McMahon, Levesque actually sought advice from Undertaker about revealing the relationship to the locker room.

"I had gone to Taker at one point because Taker for me was always kind of the constant in the locker room and I really respected his opinion," says Levesque. "I asked Taker, 'Dude, can I talk to you about something personal?' We had a really good relationship at that point. We talked about it, and this was at the point in time when nobody knew but everybody kind of knew. I said, 'Clearly, you've seen this thing with me and Steph.' He responded, 'You would have to be an idiot not to.' And I'm like, 'I just need advice on this.' Taker said, 'Well, you got to understand what you're playing with. It's a little bit of fire if it doesn't go well and it's not an amicable split. Then where are you? Are you willing to make that gamble?' And I said, 'Yeah, there are perception issues: the perception of me and my career, the perception of Steph and her career and the company as a whole, and Vince and his perception and how it affects him and the business and all that.' Taker thought about it for a long time, but at the end of it he said, 'You know what? Fuck it. Fuck all of them. It's nobody's business but yours and hers. You know who you are; you know what you do; you know how you work with everybody. The day everybody finds out about this, you will become the piece of shit that only got to where he got to because he was banging the boss's daughter. And there will always be an asterisk next to your career and everything you do going forward and that it was all given to you for no reason. But you know who you are and how hard you work.' He laid all that stuff out to me and then concluded, 'You have nothing to prove to anybody—to me, to Vince, to anybody—about your passion and all the other things for the business. Go for it.' So that was a big thing."

STEPHANIE TALKS WEDDING ANGLE

"The whole wedding ceremony was very surreal. I actually had my real-life friends. Most of them wound up being my bridesmaids in my actual wedding. So they were all there for the fake wedding first. I think it unfolded pretty well. I don't think anyone expected it. Before the wedding ceremony began, Mr. McMahon, my dad, came out and said that if anyone interrupted this wedding ceremony that wasn't family, they'd be fired on the spot. Triple H came out in his tuxedo t-shirt and leather jacket and interrupted the wedding and said, 'Hold on a second. You can't fire me. I got something to show you, dad.' And he unveiled the footage of the drive-through wedding chapel. It was, I think, pretty well received."

"Ironically, by the way, someone gave us the drive-through wedding chapel marriage certificate in a frame and I still have it. We have it in our office in our house."

THE MONDAY NIGHT WAR

WCW Nitro versus *Monday Night Raw* wasn't just a fight for ratings; it was a fight for survival.

"Ted Turner made a commitment to put *Nitro* on TNT because Turner wanted to beat McMahon," says Jim Ross. "Turner wanted his company to be the best company just like he wanted the Braves to be competitive and win the World Series. He wanted his wrestling group to go from a strong regional company to the best national brand, and he was spending big money and bringing in a lot of established stars to help facilitate that. They decided to put a wrestling show on in primetime, and it was all about competing head-to-head with WWE."

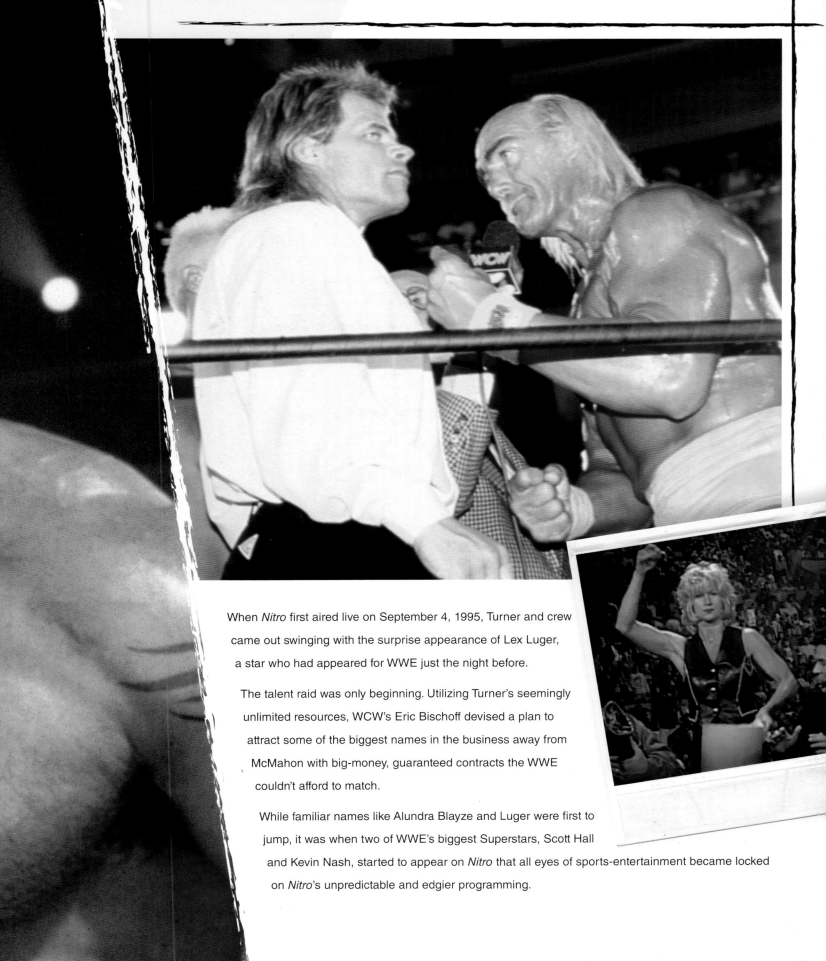

When *Nitro* first aired live on September 4, 1995, Turner and crew came out swinging with the surprise appearance of Lex Luger, a star who had appeared for WWE just the night before.

The talent raid was only beginning. Utilizing Turner's seemingly unlimited resources, WCW's Eric Bischoff devised a plan to attract some of the biggest names in the business away from McMahon with big-money, guaranteed contracts the WWE couldn't afford to match.

While familiar names like Alundra Blayze and Luger were first to jump, it was when two of WWE's biggest Superstars, Scott Hall and Kevin Nash, started to appear on *Nitro* that all eyes of sports-entertainment became locked on *Nitro*'s unpredictable and edgier programming.

"... It was pretty clever, quite frankly, on the part of whoever's idea it was, probably Hogan, to be able to position them as invading WCW. So I thought, 'Uh oh, now I'm really in trouble.'"

—Vince McMahon

"I was expecting them to debut, but not as their WWE characters Razor Ramon and Diesel," says McMahon. "So that was, I felt, infringing on our trademarks, and I didn't like it. I subsequently sued Turner. But it was pretty clever, quite frankly, on the part of whoever's idea it was, probably Hogan, to be able to position them as invading WCW. So I thought, 'Uh oh, now I'm really in trouble.'"

The fact that *Nitro* was airing live while *Raw* was taped weeks in advance enabled Bischoff to go on air and read the *Raw* results before they were even shown. McMahon found himself on the ropes early, with many questioning whether or not his organization was destined for bankruptcy.

"Many of us were taking pay cuts because the WWE at that point in time was being challenged to make payroll," says Jim Ross. "The business was just flat."

"It was that bad that we were going to mortgage our quote 'retirement home,'" says McMahon. "Those are some times you don't forget."

While *Nitro* was catching fire thanks to Hall and Nash forming the New World Order (nWo) with a now heel "Hollywood" Hulk Hogan, the WWE creative team realized that they needed to quickly change direction.

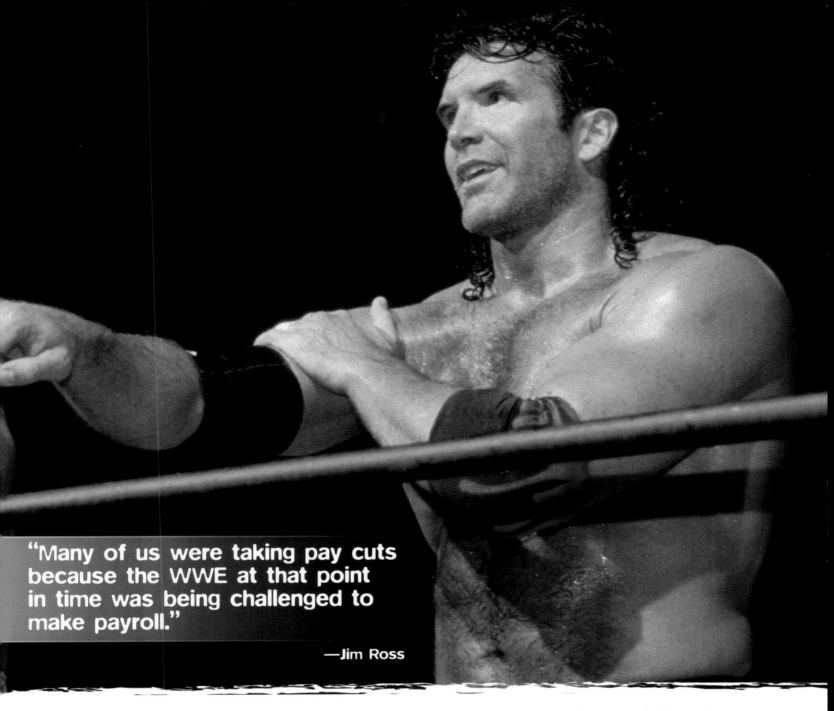

"Many of us were taking pay cuts because the WWE at that point in time was being challenged to make payroll."

—Jim Ross

"The star power at the time was somewhat stagnant," says Ross. "It was a transition period where a lot of great stars had reached an unproductive age due to injuries, a laissez-faire attitude, or from being worn out. They had found their ever-dangerous comfort zone, so we faced a situation where we needed to make changes and bring in new talent. Guys like Steve Austin, The Rock, Mankind, Triple H, and a reinvented Undertaker were given the chance to take WWE in a new direction. The talent we had at the time was all attitude, and that's the direction our show was headed."

While Ross was confident in the new crop of WWE talent, the ratings didn't lie. *Nitro* beat *Raw* 83 weeks in a row, thanks to the star power of the nWo, a concept that Bischoff originally saw play out in New Japan Pro Wrestling and then adopted for American audiences.

"The nWo was such a novel idea," says Ross. "It was an idea that had been used in Japan very successfully. The general American wrestling fan didn't know anything about what was going on in Japan, so Bischoff took a tried and true deal, cast it well, and it worked."

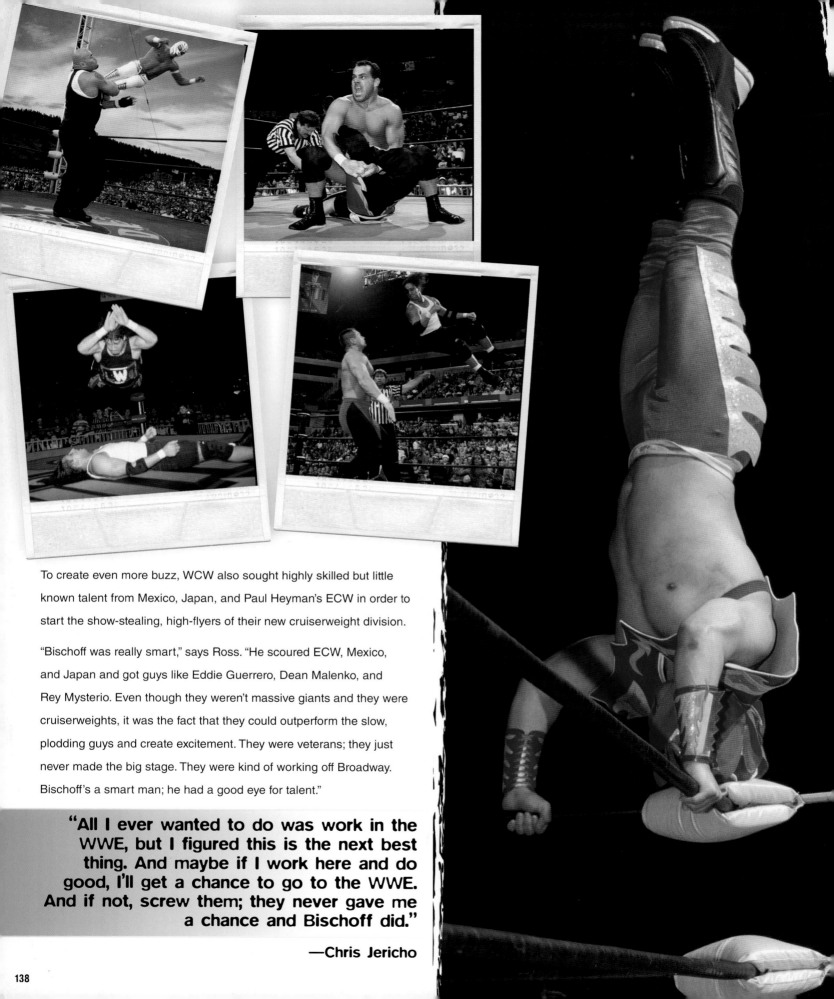

To create even more buzz, WCW also sought highly skilled but little known talent from Mexico, Japan, and Paul Heyman's ECW in order to start the show-stealing, high-flyers of their new cruiserweight division.

"Bischoff was really smart," says Ross. "He scoured ECW, Mexico, and Japan and got guys like Eddie Guerrero, Dean Malenko, and Rey Mysterio. Even though they weren't massive giants and they were cruiserweights, it was the fact that they could outperform the slow, plodding guys and create excitement. They were veterans; they just never made the big stage. They were kind of working off Broadway. Bischoff's a smart man; he had a good eye for talent."

"All I ever wanted to do was work in the WWE, but I figured this is the next best thing. And maybe if I work here and do good, I'll get a chance to go to the WWE. And if not, screw them; they never gave me a chance and Bischoff did."

—Chris Jericho

BIG SHOW ON ERIC BISCHOFF'S PERSONALITY

"Bischoff was a really weird cat. I didn't like him much at all in WCW. He was like a kid that got his dad's pistol and was threatening everyone else in the neighborhood or a kid that got his dad's AMEX. He threw money at the problem and had a limitless bank account, so they were able to do great things as far as the amount of money they would spend on talent. Bischoff could be a dick. I know that Vince can be an asshole too, don't get me wrong. You catch Vince on a bad day, you learn to check Vince's moods and go the other way. I'd have to say all in all, Vince treats people with a lot more respect. He knows the crew guys, he knows the camera guys, he knows the grip guys, and he knows the truck drivers. And Bischoff wasn't like that. I can't tell you how many times I've heard production people come up to ask Bischoff something and he'd say, 'Who are you and why are you talking to me?' He was such an arrogant ass, but he had ideas and visions."

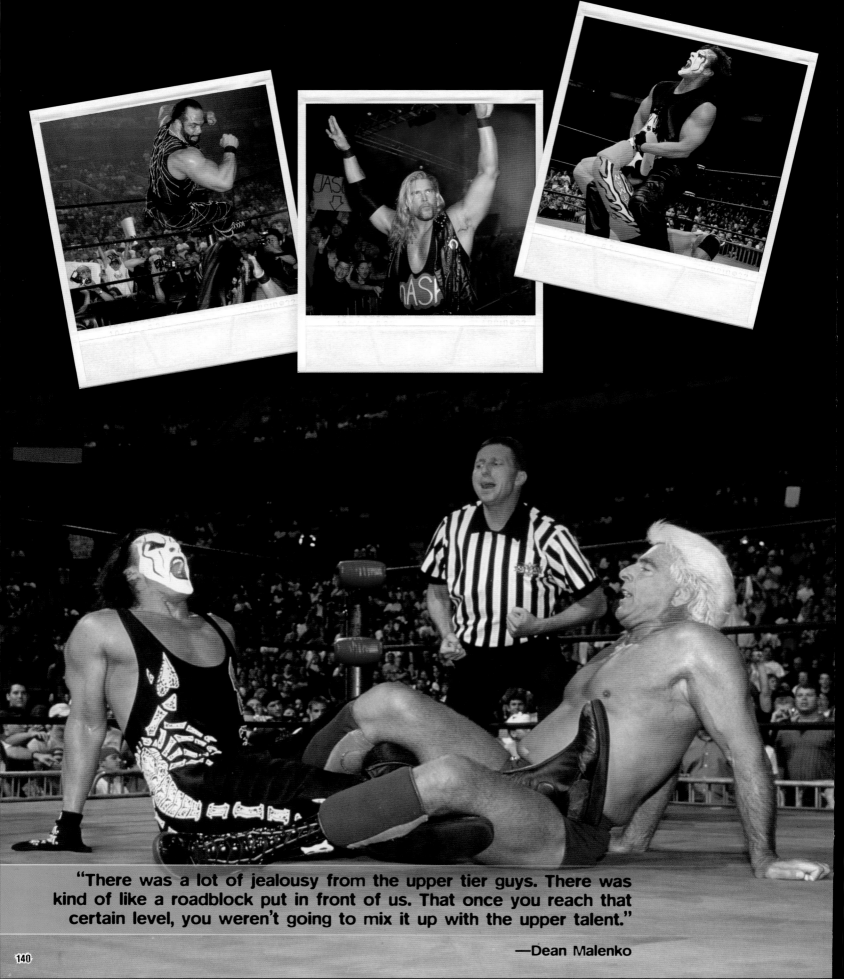

"There was a lot of jealousy from the upper tier guys. There was kind of like a roadblock put in front of us. That once you reach that certain level, you weren't going to mix it up with the upper talent."

—Dean Malenko

"I thought it was amazing because I had never worked in the states before at that level," remembers Chris Jericho. "I worked in ECW and Smoky Mountain, and here I am in TBS headquarters in Atlanta meeting with Eric Bischoff. I was just so excited. All I ever wanted to do was work in the WWE, but I figured this is the next best thing. And maybe if I work here and do good, I'll get a chance to go to the WWE. And if not, screw them; they never gave me a chance and Bischoff did. So when I first got there, it was the most amazing thing ever. Meanwhile, I was like the lowest of the food chain guys, but pretty soon I started to see how it was and that the guys on top pretty much ran the show. There was no one guy. There was no Vince McMahon. There was Bischoff who listened to Hogan, Nash, Hall, Savage, and Sting. All the guys had their own opinions, and guys like me that were just kind of like the bottom feeders were pretty much treated as such. It didn't take too long—maybe a month and a half or two—for me to start thinking, 'This isn't as cool as Japan. I don't know if I like this much.' And it kind of started going downhill from there."

141

Jericho wasn't the only star feeling disgruntled over the backstage ego-trips and mismanagement behind the scenes of *Nitro*.

"In any business, there is a certain jealousy that goes around the locker room," says Dean Malenko. "I think that was beginning once the recognition of the cruiserweights really started coming full bloom and they really started making a name for themselves. There was a lot of jealousy from the upper tier guys. There was kind of like a roadblock put in front of us. That once you reach that certain level, you weren't going to mix it up with the upper talent. There was a lot of animosity with a lot of guys, but I was always taught that once you're in the ring with your opponent, do the best you can. We felt, at some times, very stagnant. Like, this is as far as we are going to go. Unfortunately, management wouldn't let us get past a certain level, which was sometimes a little confusing and a little depressing. But it's what it was and we kind of took it with a grain of salt as best we could. But toward the latter part of it, it started getting very irritating."

"The nWo and WCW was so hot," says Arn Anderson, "and once the ratings flip-flopped and we started to dominate, there was a high. It was a feeling of success, but it got to the point of greed. We had to win every quarter hour, every segment of every show. The guys that were smart enough and knew the business and saw what was happening would try to slow it down. They would try to talk to Eric and say, 'Let's try to get a couple or three weeks out of this.' When Sting and Hulk Hogan have a one-week promotion and a one-off, the first time they ever wrestled in Macon Georgia? Now you tell me, who's the dumbass that put that on the air? I'm sorry—one-week promotion, dream match of a lifetime, and then a one-off. You look at situations like that, and you know at that moment in time, this is a mistake, it's a huge one. But you didn't have the clout to stop it, and you could see the destruction already starting to take place when the company was at its hottest if you knew what you were looking for."

While WCW continued to ride high thanks to the nWo storyline and the introduction of the yet-to-be-defeated Goldberg, WWE was building momentum with their slew of young stars who dared to do just about anything to capture attention and remote-control clicks.

"I was aware of what the nWo were doing, but I didn't watch much because my philosophy is to take care of your own business," says McMahon. "I had to watch our business even closer. In the other aspect, I did learn a few things by watching their show in terms of how to deal with commercial breaks. They would have had that information because of the extraordinary amount of research that they would have done. We didn't have those resources at the time, but they were making a lot of noise and it made us compete all the stronger."

"We had a better product and I thought we always did," says McMahon. It took the audience a while to realize that, and there were a number of weeks where WCW beat WWE in the television ratings. That's all well and good, but their live events suffered. They didn't understand the business that they were really in. We understood that, eventually, if we could hang in there long enough, those talents would burn themselves out. They did, and we hung in there, which was very difficult at times. But we hung in there until we had a better mousetrap, and the audience gravitated back to us."

CHRIS JERICHO DISCUSSES WCW'S RATINGS DOMINANCE

"I had a sense of pride because I worked my ass off every night and so did my friends and so did my peers. And even when no one else cared, I did care. I cared about my matches. But I didn't care about beating the WWE because all I wanted to do was go to the WWE in the first place. I wanted to be on *Raw* because it was cool. Even though they might've been losing the ratings, the stuff they were doing was way better than the stuff we were doing. The WWE main event guys delivered: Bret Hart, Shawn Michaels, Undertaker, Steve Austin. They put on great main event matches. Their undercard was crap. Ours was the opposite. Our undercard worked their butts off and provided great matches, and the main events sucked. Fine. No one cares enough about undercard guys anyways. I didn't care about the undercard guys in WWE. I just cared about the main event guys who were putting on five-star matches. That's where I wanted to be. So did I take pride in beating them? No, because I didn't feel like I was a part of the team. And plus, I knew just by the attitude and the fact that they never brought anyone else new into the fold on top that it wouldn't last forever. I knew it. It wasn't rocket science. The only people that didn't know it were the guys running WCW."

"... Once the ratings flip-flopped and we started to dominate, there was a high. It was a feeling of success, but it got to the point of greed."

—Arn Anderson

This was due in large part to McMahon himself, who transformed into the trademark villain of the era, putting his body on the line portraying the cocky Mr. McMahon character that the wrestling world loved to hate. A character that also helped give rise to the anti-hero Stone Cold Steve Austin. By April 6, 1998, the tide turned and WWE *Raw* once again found itself on top of the ratings.

It didn't get any better for WCW, as so many new members joined the nWo, they splintered the group off into various factions like the Wolfpac and nWo Black & White. But it was too late, and the main draw of the show was now looking as tired as its dated stars.

Meanwhile, fresh faces like The Rock and D-Generation X continued to carry *Raw* to new heights, thanks to the cocky combination of charisma, catchphrases, and crotch chops, all of which began to take hold in American pop culture. Add to that the fact that younger, up-and-coming stars like Chris Jericho and Eddie Guerrero made the jump from WCW to WWE, and *Raw* was hitting on all cylinders. As WCW tried to right the ship by firing Bischoff and replacing him with former WWE creative writer Vince Russo (responsible for many of the Attitude Era storylines), WWE continued to roll with outstanding ratings. Russo tried to bring more edge to the WCW product, but instead, his "Crash TV" style of Jerry Springer booking only led *Nitro* to collapse to the point WCW eventually brought Bischoff back into the creative mix.

"I didn't like Vince. I still don't like Vince," says Goldberg. "I always thought Vince was a plant from the WWE. I think he brought some stuff to the table that had no place on national TV. I don't have one good thing to say about him, period."

Goldberg continues, "When the two companies were going head to head and pulling the ratings, trying to one-up each other every week, you try to push the envelope," reflects Goldberg. "You try to cross that line to get extra viewers, whether it's putting more T&A on the show or more adult-orientated language or violence. That was kind of the time when all of that stuff was brought in, I believe, when Vince came down. I am a firm believer that wrestling was made for kids to watch Saturday night with their grandmothers. From generation to generation it changes, and it can't be as wholesome of a product as it once was, but who the hell are we to say that it can't be? I thought he brought a lot of crap, a lot of ornaments to be hung on our product that were distasteful, and I think he had an ulterior motive at the end of the day. I couldn't stand him."

In the end, though, it wasn't the shoddy booking or backstage backbiting that ruined WCW; it was the January 2001 merger between Time Warner and AOL. Due to the merger, Ted Turner no longer had the unchecked power to spend millions on talent, and WCW was eventually sold to McMahon and the WWE for pennies on the dollar. This lead to the final *Nitro*, a night where Shane McMahon appeared on the show to declare himself as the (storyline) new owner of WCW.

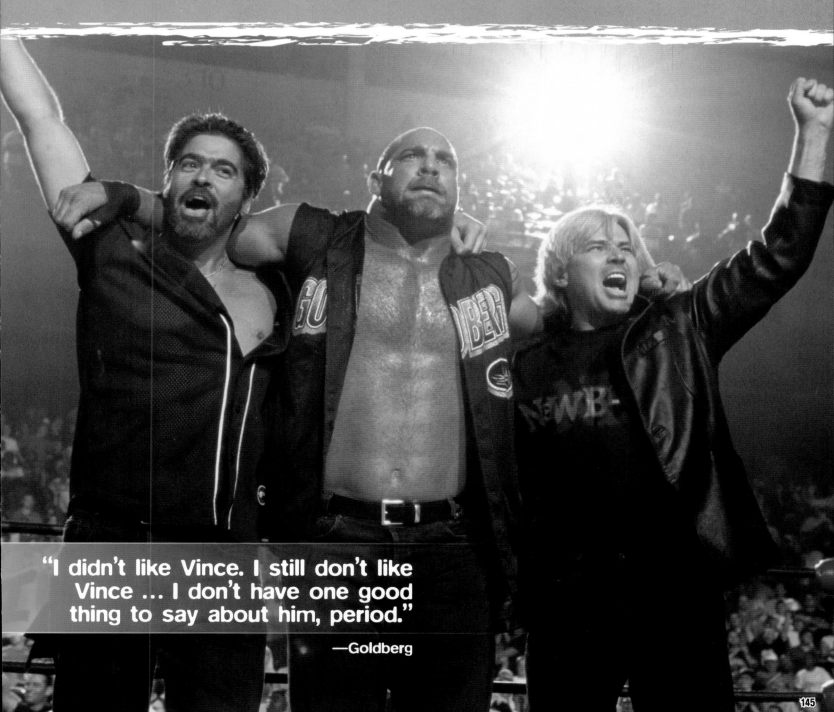

"I didn't like Vince. I still don't like Vince ... I don't have one good thing to say about him, period."

—Goldberg

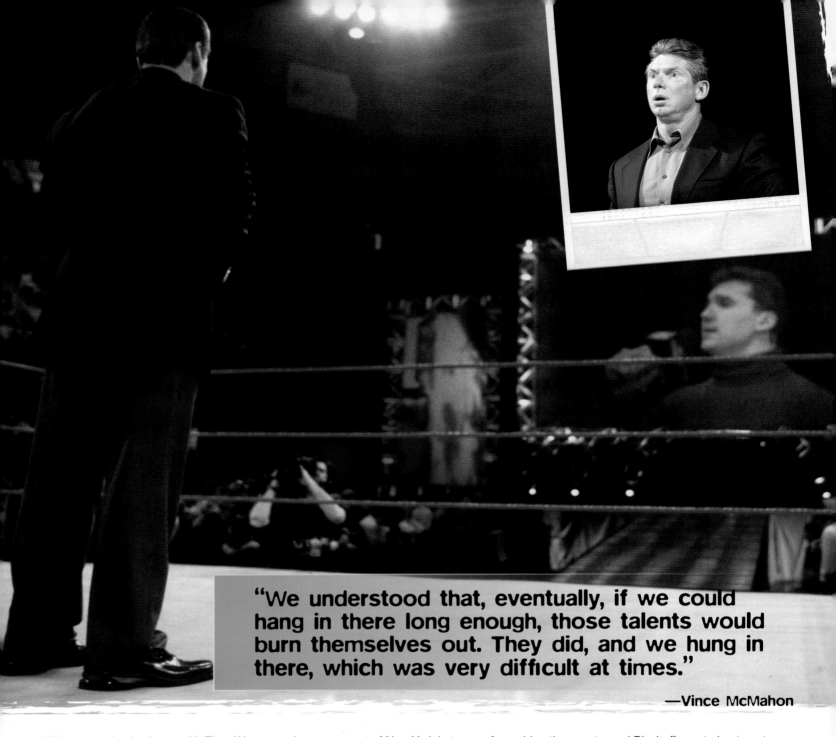

> "We understood that, eventually, if we could hang in there long enough, those talents would burn themselves out. They did, and we hung in there, which was very difficult at times."
>
> —Vince McMahon

"We were doing business with Time Warner and someone out of New York in terms of acquiring the assets, and Bischoff was trying to get a group of investors together and trying as well to secure some sort of time on Turner's networks, which would not have worked," says McMahon. "Bischoff could have bought the assets, but what do you do with them? We could do something with them. Bischoff's investors wisely dropped out on him. I don't know what he could have done with it because he would be back in the syndication business and have to take it somewhere else; it would have been difficult for them to make that a go."

"I didn't feel any ego boost of, 'way to go Vince, you crushed them, and now you own them,' and all of that. I look at it as business as usual. His asset was available, we got what I thought was a great deal, and we knew what we could do with it. We also knew that the television contract was being terminated in a short period of time. We were actually on both the Turner Network for maybe just weeks, as well as USA, and it was kind of cool the way we did that where Shane shows up running WCW head-to-head again. And all of a sudden, WCW pops up on our WWE trons and… What is this! We were able to go back and forth, which I thought the audience did not know was going to happen. It was a pretty cool night."

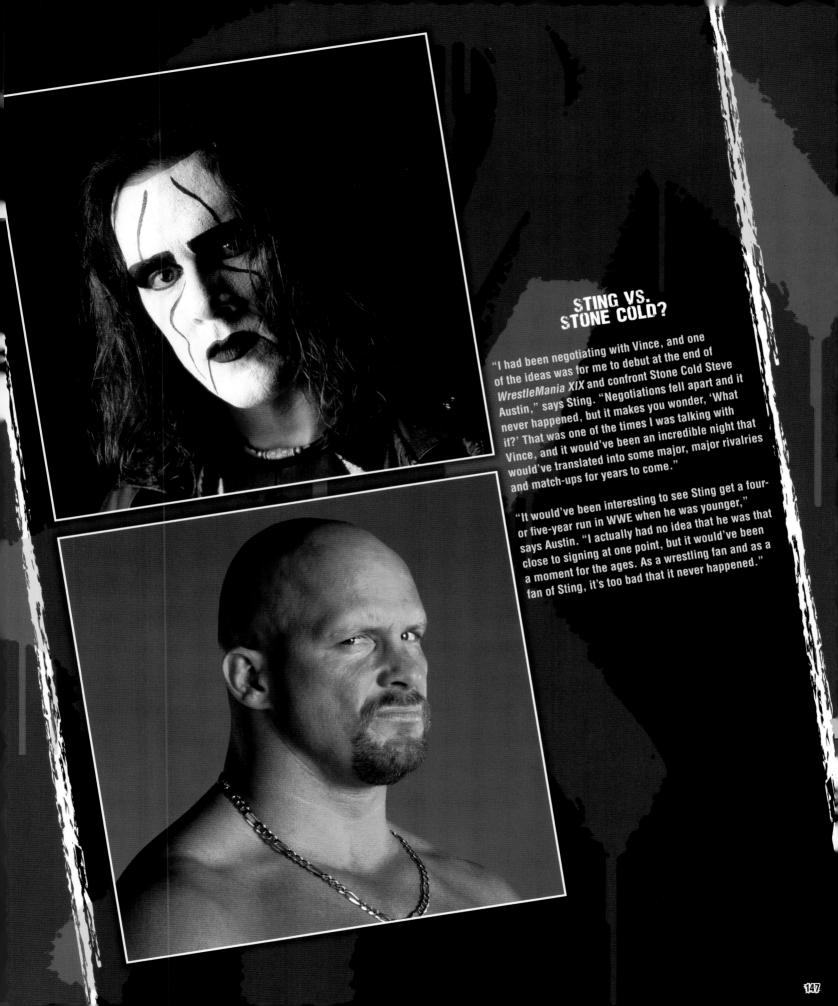

STING VS. STONE COLD?

"I had been negotiating with Vince, and one of the ideas was for me to debut at the end of *WrestleMania XIX* and confront Stone Cold Steve Austin," says Sting. "Negotiations fell apart and it never happened, but it makes you wonder, 'What if?' That was one of the times I was talking with Vince, and it would've been an incredible night that would've translated into some major, major rivalries and match-ups for years to come."

"It would've been interesting to see Sting get a four- or five-year run in WWE when he was younger," says Austin. "I actually had no idea that he was that close to signing at one point, but it would've been a moment for the ages. As a wrestling fan and as a fan of Sting, it's too bad that it never happened."

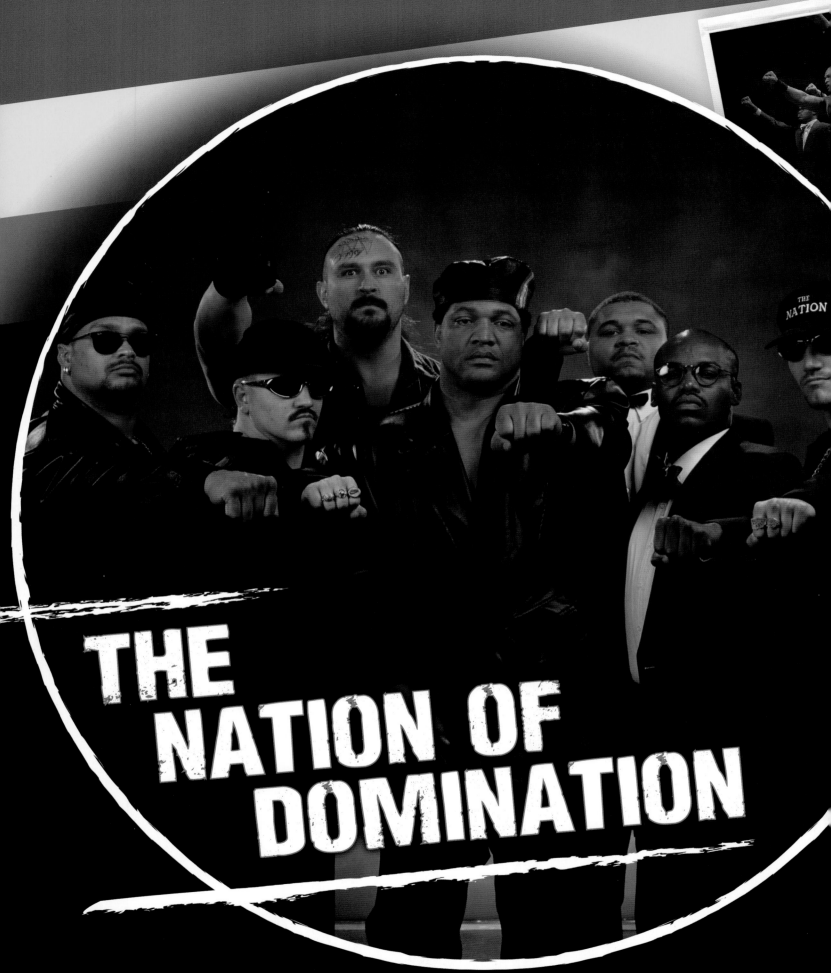

THE NATION OF DOMINATION

Ask any WWE Superstar about The Nation of Domination and you'll hear the same reply: "They are the most underrated stable in the history of sports-entertainment." Then again, what else can be said about a group that featured everyone from former WCW Heavyweight Champion Farooq to the first-ever simultaneous European and Intercontinental Champion D-Lo Brown to the most electrifying man in sports-entertainment history (not to mention eight-time WWE Champion) The Rock.

But it wasn't always main events and championships for The Nation. In fact, when the stable started in 1996, featuring Farooq (Ron Simmons), Crush, Savio Vega, and manager Clarence Mason, the group had a lack of chemistry that appeared destined for jobberville.

"No disrespect to the first guys, but that's not The Nation people remember," says D-Lo Brown, who started as one of the stable's bodyguards but quickly found himself inside the ring. "When people weren't buying Farooq, Crush, and Savio as a group, they decided to split up. Each guy then became the leader of his own faction, igniting the gang warfare seen on *Raw* among The Nation (led by Farooq), Crush's Disciples of Apocalypse, and Savio's Los Boricuas."

With Crush and Vega quickly pushed out of the group, Farooq recruited new members ranging from D-Lo Brown and Kama "The Ultimate Fighting Machine" (formerly known as Papa Shango) to Mark Henry and The Rock.

"I'm joining The Nation. It's not a white thing. It's not a black thing. It's a me kicking your ass thing. And I'm a lot of things, but I promise you, 'sucks' is not one of them."

WE ARE THE NATION

Every character who ever joined or was associated with The Nation of Domination:

Farooq

Crush

Savio Vega

Clarence Mason

PG-13
(J.C. Ice and Wolfie D)

D-Lo Brown

Ahmed Johnson

Kama
(The Godfather)

The Rock

Mark Henry

Owen Hart

"When The Nation started, the guys standing in the background wearing suits were just friends of Clarence Mason. They weren't really wrestlers," says Brown. "They needed a guy in a suit who could interfere in the matches and bump around, so that's when Jim Cornette and Jim Ross called me for a tryout.

"After they realized that I could be a serviceable hand, I moved from a guy in a suit to an in-ring participant. I was wrestling at all of the house shows, so that's when they got the idea to do the gang warfare and split the Nation of Domination into three factions with the DOA and Los Boriquas, along with The Nation and DX rivalry.

"The concept there was just trying to peak as much interest into these four factions. But I remember when things really changed for the group, and that's when we added The Rock."

"A lot of the guys who came to form the Nation were all talented," says Ron Simmons, "but they lacked direction. They lacked a gimmick people could latch onto. Even with The Rock, they wanted him in a grass skirt jumping off the top rope, but that wasn't him. At that point, they asked me about The Rock joining The Nation, and I thought it was a great idea because it would give him a platform to speak, and it would give him the legitimacy he lacked when he first debuted."

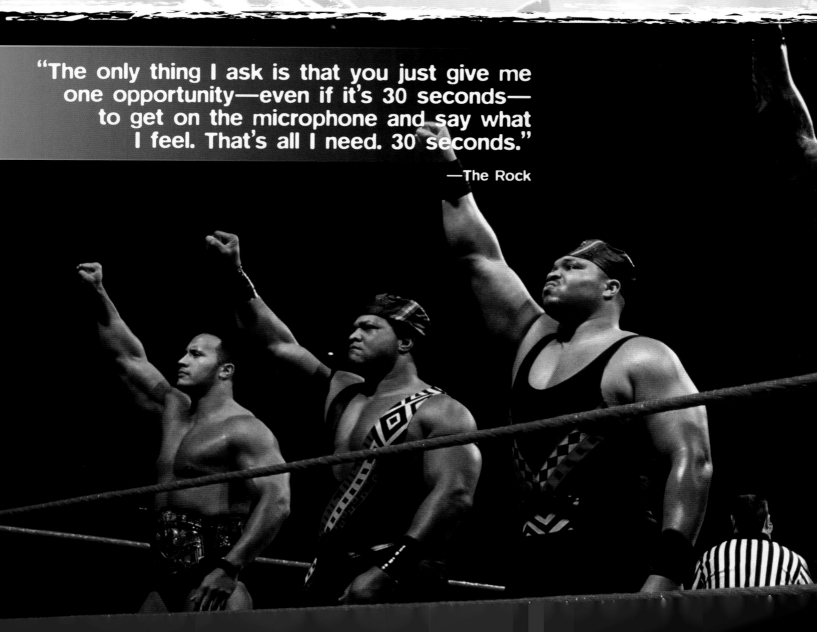

"The only thing I ask is that you just give me one opportunity—even if it's 30 seconds—to get on the microphone and say what I feel. That's all I need. 30 seconds."

—The Rock

"I got hurt, and then I was able to take the summer off," recalls The Rock. "I remember getting a phone call, and Jim Ross said, 'How do you feel about joining the Nation of Domination? We're going to turn you into a bad guy. You're going to become a heel.' I said, 'I love it. Love it. The only thing I ask is that you just give me one opportunity—even if it's 30 seconds—to get on the microphone and say what I feel. That's all I need. 30 seconds.'"

Ross went to Vince McMahon with the request, and The Rock got his 30 seconds to prove himself.

"One night, I said, 'I'm joining The Nation. It's not a white thing. It's not a black thing. It's a me kicking your ass thing. And I'm a lot of things, but I promise you, 'sucks' is not one of them,'" explains The Rock, as he remembers the chants of "Rocky sucks!" from the crowd. "And just in that, I was able to be myself. From then on, we shot out like a rocket."

"What people don't realize about our group is that once the five of us were together, we were not only tight on screen, but we were all great friends off screen as well, and that really helped add to the chemistry," explains Mark Henry. "I used to live with Rocky, and when we were on the road, all five of us would travel together. We'd constantly be coming up with ideas for catchphrases or moves—anything that would help us standout—and a lot of what you'd end up seeing on TV was created during those long car rides together."

By 1998, however, on-screen tensions escalated. The Rock's rise was palpable, and WWE decided it was time to see what this up-and-coming star could do as the leader of his own faction.

"It worked out great," says Brown, "because after Ron and Rock clashed on screen, Ron was able to join the Acolytes while The Rock was given the chance to really shine front and center. This was one of those moments where everyone benefited from the switch."

But The Rock's leadership wasn't the only change. The group shortened their name to The Nation, Kama transformed into The Godfather, D-Lo Brown began strutting around the ring with a head wobble that would make Merton Hanks jealous, and Owen Hart even joined the ranks.

"Once Rocky took over, we were all able to be more like ourselves on screen," says Brown. "And the crowd really ate it up."

As The Nation climbed the card, they began what would become their signature rivalry against another group of brash and cocky superstars, D-Generation X.

"When the Attitude Era was at its peak, you had The Nation versus D-X all up and down the card. It was more than half the show," says Henry. "You might have The Rock versus Triple H as the main event, but just below that, you had me and D-Lo taking on The Outlaws, or D-Lo versus X-Pac, and The Godfather versus Billy Gunn, or me versus Shawn Michaels. It was a focal point of *Raw* back then, and I think a lot of people forget that."

What hasn't been forgotten is the now notorious parody skit the D-X members performed of The Nation. Each D-X Superstar portrayed a specific Nation member while really playing up their trademark mannerisms.

> "When the Attitude Era was at its peak, you had The Nation versus D-X all up and down the card. It was more than half the show."
>
> —Mark Henry

"I loved it," laughs D-Lo Brown. "Road Dogg was doing my head waggle and walking around the ring like I would, and until then, I don't think people were really catching on to what I was doing out there. But after that skit, every time I did the head waggle, people would go nuts. For me, at least, the skit really helped elevate my character."

KNOW YOUR ROLE

"When Mark Henry was first getting into The Nation," recalls Ron Simmons, "I had to remind him, yes, we're entertaining, but I'm still the leader of this group. He had just joined The Nation and we were on live TV. This was his first time on TV with us, and I had already told him what was supposed to happen. I was going to come out, I was going to give my speech, then he was supposed to arrive at a certain point. So just when I'm starting my speech at the top of the ramp, Mark Henry interrupts me. I had to stop and break out of my character. I dropped the mic down so it wouldn't come across on TV, and I turned to Henry and said, 'Listen to me, boy. You need to shut up and do what I told you. Don't say another word!' It was so funny because all of the fans really picked up on it and were like, wow, Farooq really is the leader of The Nation. The way it came off on camera really is funny when you look back on it. Mark had no idea how things worked back then. He was really green, but he learned his lesson."

THE NEW JOHNNY BENCH

"The chest protector lives in infamy to this day," says D-Lo Brown. "Fans come up to me and act like I still carry the chest protector around in my suitcase. They still want to see it! The funny thing about it is that I didn't want to wear the chest protector at all in the beginning. I thought I would be a joke. But I'll give credit to good old JR because it was his idea. He came up to me at lunch one day and was like, 'Hey D-Lo, I have this great idea I want to pitch to you.' And at the time, I was still just a suit guy in the background of The Nation, so I was looking for anything to elevate my way up the company. JR asked me if I had ever heard of Iron Mike Sharpe, and, of course, everybody remembers him for his arm that never healed. But I didn't want to do the same thing and pretend to hurt my arm. Then JR said, 'Your finish is the Frog Splash. How about we do something with your chest? You can wear a chest protector, and then when you use it for your finisher, people will hate you.' I remember looking at him and nodding my head like, 'Yeah, yeah, that sounds great.' Then as soon as he left, all I could think was, 'Man, I sure hope he forgets about that.' I thought I was going to be the laughing stock of the business, looking like Johnny Bench out there with this catcher's gear. But I went out there and they hurt my chest with Dan Severn. Then a couple of weeks later, I ran out while The Rock was wrestling Ken Shamrock, and I helped The Rock win the Intercontinental Championship by hitting the Frog Splash with the chest protector. It turned out being one of the best things to ever happen for my career. It helped separate me from everybody else on the card by making me different, and I give all props to Jim Ross for not only coming up with the idea, but for making me stick to it."

D-LO TO DX?

Was D-Lo Brown supposed to turn on the Nation and join DX? While the betrayal never happened on air, the turn is mentioned in both an official WWE trivia game and on a WWE calendar. "I have no clue if that was ever a concept or an idea, but somehow it got through on two official pieces of WWE merchandise," explains Brown. "According to all of this merchandise, I was a member of DX, but nobody ever told me about it. Fans will come up to me and ask, 'When were you a member of DX? I saw it on a calendar.' I actually still remember looking at the WWE calendar, and it said this is the day D-Lo Brown betrayed the Nation and joined DX. I was like, 'When did that happen? Somebody owes me some DX royalty money.'"

Throughout the summer, the D-X/Nation rivalry simmered, but by October 1998, The Rock's overwhelming crowd reactions had caught the attention of the creative forces backstage, and they knew it was time to turn The Rock into the company's new hero.

"What we had with The Rock was truly something special, and we knew we had to spin him out of the group in order to make him that much bigger of a star," says Jim Ross.

And that's exactly what happened as Mark Henry and D-Lo Brown teamed up for a beatdown of The Rock, turning on their former leader, and in doing so, breaking up the once mighty Nation.

"It's funny, people still come up to me and ask me when The Nation is coming back," laughs Henry. "In this business, one thing's for sure: you never know."

THE CORPORATION

"I don't like people that don't have a little bit of scoundrel in them."

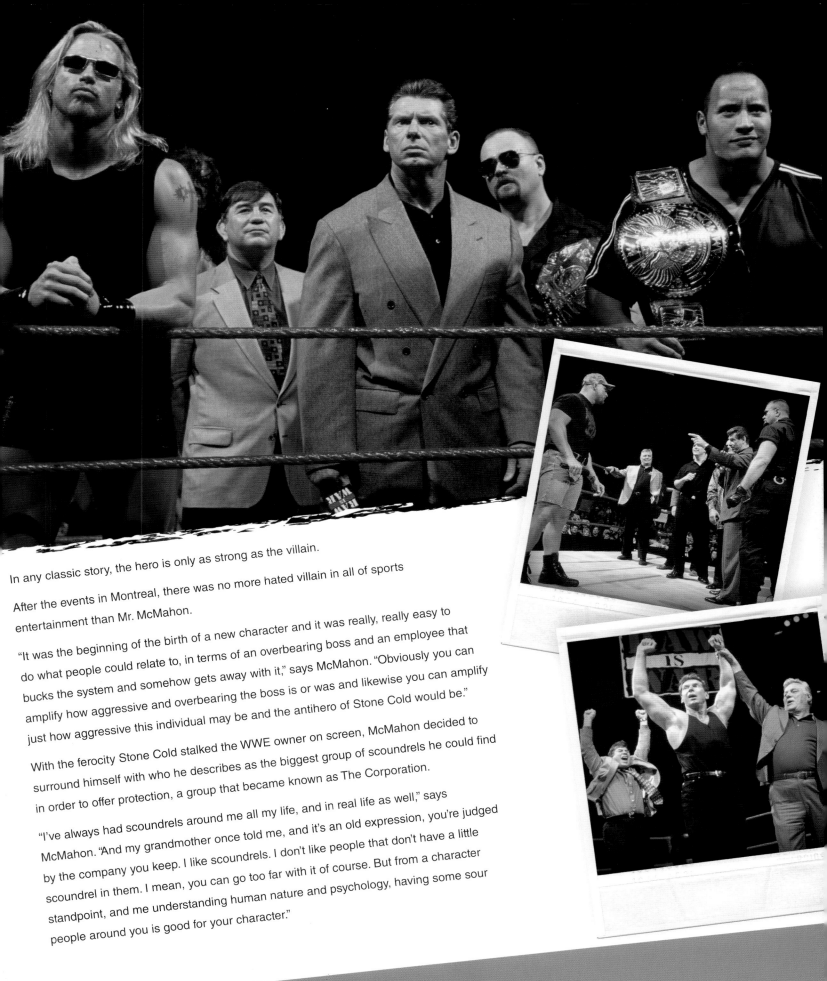

In any classic story, the hero is only as strong as the villain.

After the events in Montreal, there was no more hated villain in all of sports entertainment than Mr. McMahon.

"It was the beginning of the birth of a new character and it was really, really easy to do what people could relate to, in terms of an overbearing boss and an employee that bucks the system and somehow gets away with it," says McMahon. "Obviously you can amplify how aggressive and overbearing the boss is or was and likewise you can amplify just how aggressive this individual may be and the antihero of Stone Cold would be."

With the ferocity Stone Cold stalked the WWE owner on screen, McMahon decided to surround himself with who he describes as the biggest group of scoundrels he could find in order to offer protection, a group that became known as The Corporation.

"I've always had scoundrels around me all my life, and in real life as well," says McMahon. "And my grandmother once told me, and it's an old expression, you're judged by the company you keep. I like scoundrels. I don't like people that don't have a little scoundrel in them. I mean, you can go too far with it of course. But from a character standpoint, and me understanding human nature and psychology, having some sour people around you is good for your character."

STONE COLD VINCE MCMAHON?!

"It's ironic that really Stone Cold Steve Austin, that character, is really Vince McMahon. So I have a vast background of divergence in so many areas. I knew I was the redneck and I was the guy to buck the system and I was the guy to tell the boss to go to hell. That was me in real life, and so it's easy to relate to that on both sides because I know what I didn't like and I know how I was treated and it's like, 'You're not going to treat me that way. You're not going to treat me that way without me saying something or doing something the best I can.' That was such an easy story to be able to tell because in real life it was flipped because Vince McMahon really wasn't Mr. McMahon, even though some people think I really still am. I was really Stone Cold Steve Austin."

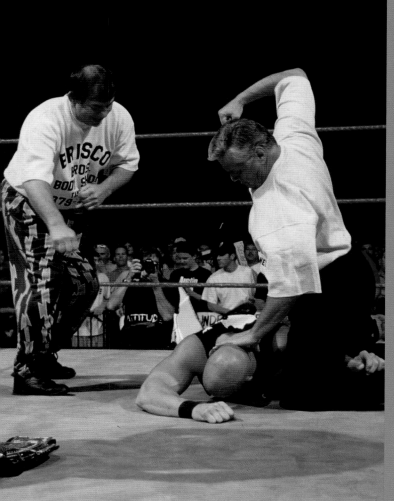

McMahon's initial group of scoundrels consisted of Gerald Brisco and Pat Patterson (The Corporate Stooges), as well as Commissioner Slaughter and Big Boss Man.

The Corporation's biggest move, however, was the recruitment of The Rock, who turned his back on "The People" to become "The Corporate Champ." In fact, with The Rock as WWE Champion, new recruit Ken Shamrock as Intercontinental Champion, and Big Boss Man as the Hardcore Champion, The Corporation proved to have not only the political stroke to seemingly accomplish anything, but also all of the gold to back it up.

Besides Austin, the faction also famously clashed with the likes of Mankind and DX. When The Corporation began fighting against Undertaker and his Ministry of Darkness after Undertaker became obsessed with Stephanie McMahon (even kidnapping her at the end of *Backlash 1999*), Shane McMahon stepped in to kick his dad out of the group, claiming Vince was only worried about Stephanie's safety and not what was good for the company. Shane then went on to relieve Brisco and Patterson of their duties, replacing them with his own group of stooges, The Mean Street Posse, a move that led to a wild stooge brawl (and one of the most viewed segments in the history of *Raw*).

"Those kids were good kids, but they were not good wrestlers," Patterson says of the Posse. "It was dangerous working with them; you never knew what they were going to come up with in the ring. They were really worried; they didn't want to hurt us because we were old timers in there doing our thing. They did their best to protect us, but I'm going to tell you something we did take care of: We let them know who was boss, and it was Patterson and Brisco. That was a fun era in those days. I really enjoyed that with those kids. People were really behind us out there. They really liked Patterson and Brisco."

Eventually, The Corporation merged with Undertaker's Ministry of Darkness to form the all-powerful Corporate Ministry, even bringing Mr. McMahon back into the fold when it was revealed that the WWE owner had been pulling the strings the whole time as the group's "Higher Power."

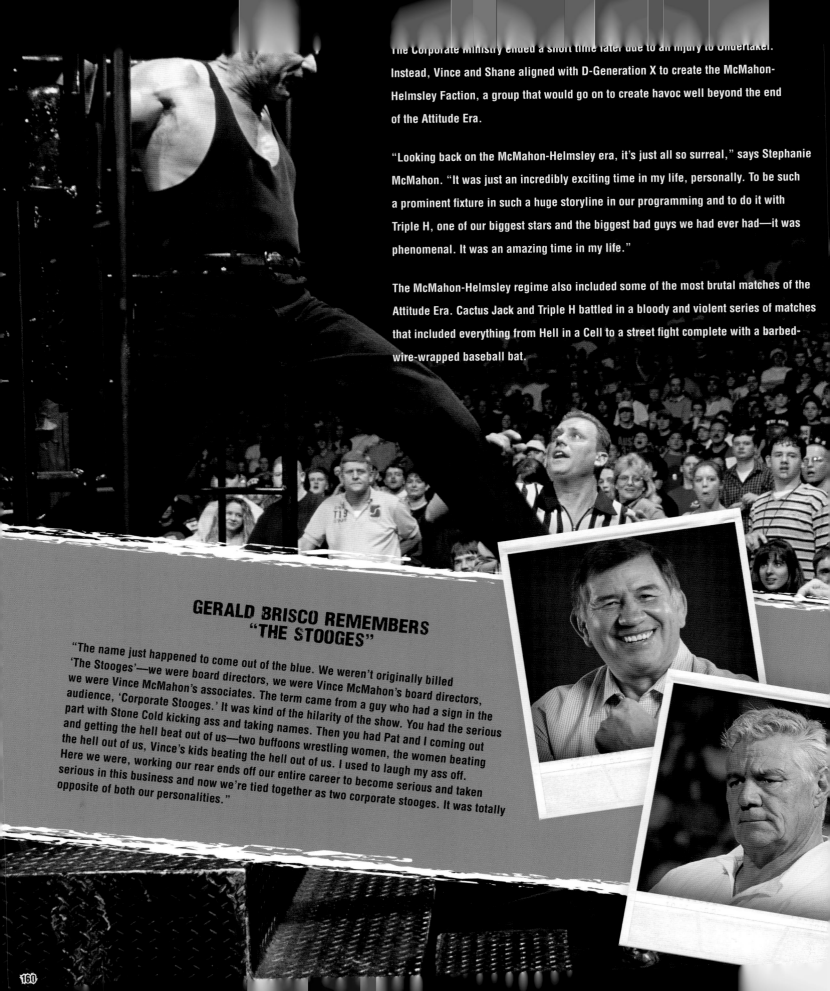

The Corporate Ministry ended a short time later due to an injury to Undertaker. Instead, Vince and Shane aligned with D-Generation X to create the McMahon-Helmsley Faction, a group that would go on to create havoc well beyond the end of the Attitude Era.

"Looking back on the McMahon-Helmsley era, it's just all so surreal," says Stephanie McMahon. "It was just an incredibly exciting time in my life, personally. To be such a prominent fixture in such a huge storyline in our programming and to do it with Triple H, one of our biggest stars and the biggest bad guys we had ever had—it was phenomenal. It was an amazing time in my life."

The McMahon-Helmsley regime also included some of the most brutal matches of the Attitude Era. Cactus Jack and Triple H battled in a bloody and violent series of matches that included everything from Hell in a Cell to a street fight complete with a barbed-wire-wrapped baseball bat.

GERALD BRISCO REMEMBERS "THE STOOGES"

"The name just happened to come out of the blue. We weren't originally billed 'The Stooges'—we were board directors, we were Vince McMahon's board directors, we were Vince McMahon's associates. The term came from a guy who had a sign in the audience, 'Corporate Stooges.' It was kind of the hilarity of the show. You had the serious part with Stone Cold kicking ass and taking names. Then you had Pat and I coming out and getting the hell beat out of us—two buffoons wrestling women, the women beating the hell out of us, Vince's kids beating the hell out of us. I used to laugh my ass off. Here we were, working our rear ends off our entire career to become serious and taken serious in this business and now we're tied together as two corporate stooges. It was totally opposite of both our personalities."

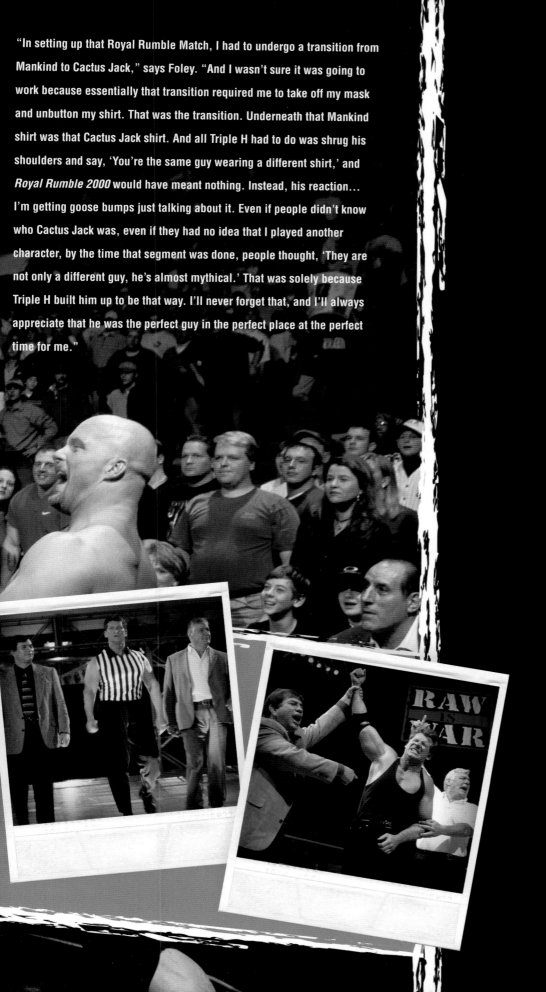

"In setting up that Royal Rumble Match, I had to undergo a transition from Mankind to Cactus Jack," says Foley. "And I wasn't sure it was going to work because essentially that transition required me to take off my mask and unbutton my shirt. That was the transition. Underneath that Mankind shirt was that Cactus Jack shirt. And all Triple H had to do was shrug his shoulders and say, 'You're the same guy wearing a different shirt,' and *Royal Rumble 2000* would have meant nothing. Instead, his reaction… I'm getting goose bumps just talking about it. Even if people didn't know who Cactus Jack was, even if they had no idea that I played another character, by the time that segment was done, people thought, 'They are not only a different guy, he's almost mythical.' That was solely because Triple H built him up to be that way. I'll never forget that, and I'll always appreciate that he was the perfect guy in the perfect place at the perfect time for me."

CORPORATION MEMBERS

MR. MCMAHON

PAT PATTERSON

GERALD BRISCO

SGT. SLAUGHTER

BIG BOSS MAN

THE ROCK

KEN SHAMROCK

TEST

SHAWN MICHAELS

SHANE MCMAHON

CHYNA

TRIPLE H

PETE GAS

RODNEY

JOEY ABS

KANE

BIG SHOW

ATTITUDE'S UNSUNG HEROES

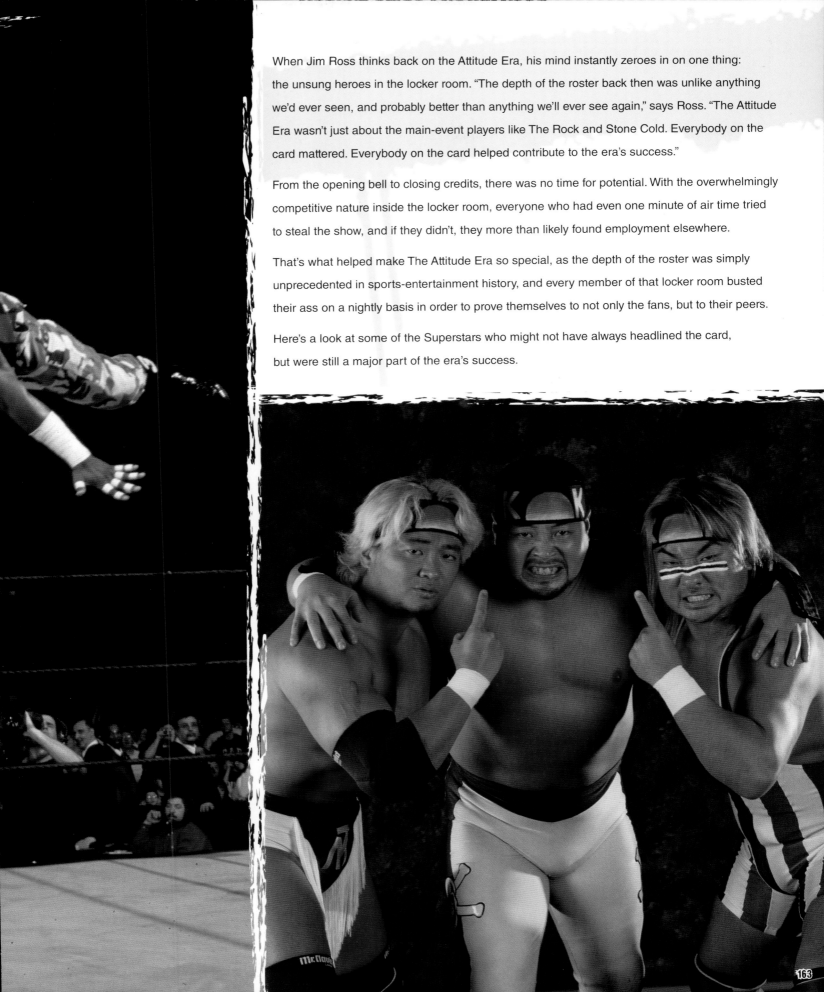

When Jim Ross thinks back on the Attitude Era, his mind instantly zeroes in on one thing: the unsung heroes in the locker room. "The depth of the roster back then was unlike anything we'd ever seen, and probably better than anything we'll ever see again," says Ross. "The Attitude Era wasn't just about the main-event players like The Rock and Stone Cold. Everybody on the card mattered. Everybody on the card helped contribute to the era's success."

From the opening bell to closing credits, there was no time for potential. With the overwhelmingly competitive nature inside the locker room, everyone who had even one minute of air time tried to steal the show, and if they didn't, they more than likely found employment elsewhere.

That's what helped make The Attitude Era so special, as the depth of the roster was simply unprecedented in sports-entertainment history, and every member of that locker room busted their ass on a nightly basis in order to prove themselves to not only the fans, but to their peers.

Here's a look at some of the Superstars who might not have always headlined the card, but were still a major part of the era's success.

KURT ANGLE

Kurt Angle was the first and only Superstar to win both an Olympic gold medal and the WWE Championship. Angle's love triangle with Stephanie McMahon and Triple H was must-see TV, and his milk truck drenching of the Alliance is a highlight to rewind and enjoy again. Angle's hardcore match against Shane McMahon at King of the Ring 2001 still holds up as one of the most violent, breathtaking bouts in WWE history.

AL SNOW

Snow was a schizophrenic who talked to a mannequin head, complete with the words "Help Me" written backwards across its forehead. He delivered some of the strangest moments of the era, including a Hardcore Match against himself. After "Head" was replaced by a Chihuahua named Pepper, The Big Bossman kidnapped the dog and then fed it to Snow.

WILLIAM REGAL

His real man's man gimmick might not have lasted long, but when Regal returned to his snobbish roots, the villain found the type of success that put his name on the WCW map. Lowlight: Regal was the first member of Vince McMahon's Kiss My Ass club.

MEAN STREET POSSE

It's attack of the sweater vests, as Pete Gas, Joey Abs, and Rodney took to the ring to watch the back of their boyhood friend Shane McMahon. Their match against Pat Patterson and Gerald Brisco is still one of the most watched segments in *Raw* history.

ODDITIES

A stable/freak show led by The Jackyl that featured everyone from The Insane Clown Posse to The Giant Silva and Kurrgan. Other members included Golga (a.k.a. Earthquake), Luna, Sable, and even George "The Animal" Steele being billed as "The Original Oddity."

VINCE RUSSO

As head writer behind the scenes, Russo is credited with many of the ideas that helped spark the Attitude Era, including Austin versus McMahon and the Brothers of Destruction, as well as introducing the world to characters like Val Venis and The Godfather. Russo signed with WCW in October, 1999, bringing his edgy style of Crash TV to *Nitro*.

GANGREL

If the entrance made the man, Gangrel would be the biggest star in the history of the business. His rise through the fiery stage, complete with goblet of blood, is still one of the coolest entrances in WWE history. The vampire's brood helped launch the WWE careers of Christian and Edge, while their blood bath routine was the stuff of Attitude Era legend.

BIG BOSS MAN

Originally debuting back in June 1988 as a foe of Hulk Hogan, Big Boss Man's Attitude reinvention included ditching his blue prison guard uniform for all-black SWAT gear in his new role as bodyguard for Vince McMahon and The Corporation. Big Boss Man's most notorious move was his invasion of Big Show's father's funeral, complete with hijacking the casket.

RIKISHI & TOO COOL

From The Worm to The Stinkface, Rikishi and Too Cool danced their way to the top of the card with memorable moves that kept the crowd grooving through every spot. Rikishi was eventually revealed as the driver who ran over Stone Cold Steve Austin during Survivor Series 1999, saying he did it to help his cousin, The Rock.

KEN SHAMROCK

Billed "The World's Most Dangerous Man," the former UFC great turned WWE Superstar made the ankle lock famous long before Kurt Angle adapted the move as his own. As a member of The Corporation, Shamrock simultaneously held both the Intercontinental and Tag Team Championship, teaming with Big Boss Man.

GERALD BRISCO & PAT PATTERSON

Patterson and Brisco were backstage producers and former Superstars turned Attitude Era "stooges" for Vince McMahon and The Corporation. The two rivaled over the Hardcore Championship after Patterson poured champagne into Brisco's eyes and then smashed him with a bottle to capture the title.

THE DUDLEY BOYZ

These former ECW greats joined WWE in 1999 and immediately made their mark with four little words: "D-Von, get the tables!" The first team ever to win the ECW, WCW, and WWE Tag Team Championships, the Dudleyz's series of matches against Edge and Christian and the Hardyz will go down as some of the best tag team action in WWE history.

MAE YOUNG & THE FABULOUS MOOLAH

The elderly duo was meant to be a comedy act, but things quickly escalated as Jeff Jarrett smashed Moolah with a guitar, and Mae Young was on the receiving end of two of the most shocking Powerbombs in WWE history, at the hands of Bubba Ray Dudley.

RIGHT TO CENSOR

When Stevie Richards began running to ringside to steal the equalizers or foreign objects from Hardcore Matches and cover up the scantily clad Divas, the Attitude crowd became infuriated, creating one of the most hated heel factions of the day. Richards even recruited the likes of Val Venis, Bull Buchanan, Ivory, and The Godfather to join his ranks as they fought to clean up WWE one degenerate at a time.

THE HOLLY COUSINS

Hardcore, Crash, and Molly Holly often debated who the toughest Holly was, but throughout the years all three proved able to throw down with the best of them. Hardcore and Crash even beat the famed Rock 'N' Sock Connection to capture WWE tag team gold. After introducing the world to the 24/7 Hardcore rules, Crash went on to win the title a staggering 22 times.

TAZZ

The former ECW Champion debuted by defeating the previously unbeaten Kurt Angle. Injuries forced a premature end to his in-ring status, leading to a full-time role as a color commentator for both *SmackDown* and ECW.

DROZ

Featured in the documentary *Beyond The Mat* as the man who could puke on command, Droz's wrestling days were cut short tragically after an in-ring accident caused him to become a quadriplegic.

GOLDUST

Goldust was Attitude before Attitude was cool, introducing the world of sports-entertainment to more adult themes while constantly pushing the envelope with his sexually ambiguous character.

STEVE BLACKMAN

"The Lethal Weapon" carried nunchaku to the ring and struck opponents with a quick-hitting martial arts style that helped make Blackman's move set unique. Blackman's hard-hitting ways were a perfect fit for WWE's 24/7 Hardcore Title, as he captured the coveted championship six times.

THE HARDY BOYZ

Seven-time tag team champs, Matt and Jeff Hardy rose to fame from meager beginnings to become one of the most popular duos in WWE history. They added Lita to the mix to become Team Xtreme, the most high-flying and death-defying trio of the Attitude Era.

D-LO BROWN

After splitting from The Nation, D-Lo Brown moved on to become the first ever simultaneous holder of both the Intercontinental and European championships. You better recognize.

X-PAC & KANE

The two-time tag team champs are best known for introducing Kane to speech, thanks to the electrolarynx. His first unaided words? "Suck it."

JEFF JARRETT

Best known for using his guitar to level his opponents, Jarrett's abusive treatment of WWE Divas led to a rivalry with Chyna. Double-J lost his

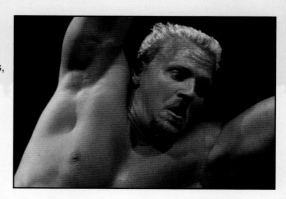

Intercontinental title to the Ninth Wonder of the World before packing up to join WCW.

EDGE & CHRISTIAN

The five-second pose, the TLC spear, their rivalry with The Hardy Boyz and the Dudley Boyz … Edge and Christian might not have been in the main event every night, but the two childhood friends and seven-time tag team champs sure knew what it was like to steal the show.

TEST & ALBERT

Otherwise known as T&A, the tag team helped introduce the world to Trish Stratus. The buxom Diva managed the duo, leading to a rivalry between T&A and Team Xtreme, giving fans a taste of the action to come between Hall of Famers Stratus and Lita.

THE GODFATHER

In a matter of life imitating art imitating life, one man parlayed his love for strip clubs to introduce a wrestling pimp persona known as The Godfather—complete with the "Ho Train"—to the world. Today, The Godfather can be found managing a club called Cheetah's in Las Vegas.

OWEN HART

One of the all-time greats, Owen Hart rivaled with Shawn Michaels and Triple H following the Montreal Screwjob. He then went on to join The Nation of Domination as The Black Hart. When the Nation broke up, Hart teamed with Jeff Jarrett, reprising his role as The Blue Blazer. He later fell to his death in a tragic accident during the Over the Edge pay-per-view event.

"SEXUAL CHOCOLATE" MARK HENRY

When The Nation split, "The World's Strongest Man" turned crowd favorite, romancing the likes of Chyna and Mae Young. This led to one of WWE history's most infamous moments, as Mae Young eventually gave birth to a hand.

VAL VENIS

From a vignette that showed him in bed with Jenna Jameson to a finishing move called the Money Shot, Val Venis' porn star gimmick was one of the most controversial gimmicks of the Attitude Era. Eventually, the porn star teamed with the pimp—The Godfather—to form the aptly named Supply and Demand.

NEW AGE OUTLAWS

From pushing Mick Foley and Terry Funk off the entrance ramp in a dumpster to joining Triple H in the new era of DX, the New Age Outlaws captured the attention of the sports-entertainment world. All the while, they added some of the best-known catch phrases of their generation to the WWE vernacular.

THE RADICALZ

Eddie Guerrero, Dean Malenko, Perry Saturn, and Chris Benoit formed this team of WCW crossovers as a real-life contract dispute led to the four Superstars joining WWE, shaking up the title scene on *Raw*.

CHRIS JERICHO

The Y2J countdown clock led to arguably the best—and most entertaining—debut as we've ever seen on *Raw*. Chris Jericho traded insults with The Rock, proving that The Great One wasn't the only master of the mic.

After Val Venis slept with Yamaguchi's wife, the stable vowed revenge, kidnapping the porn star and threatening to "choppy choppy pee pee." Luckily for Venis, he was saved by none other than John Wayne Bobbitt before castration could be completed.

Best known as her role as DX's bodyguard, the Ninth Wonder of the World also broke ground by being the first woman ever to enter the Royal Rumble Match and the first woman ever to win the Intercontinental Championship.

A.P.A.

As the Acolytes Protection Agency, former Hell's Henchmen and Acolytes Farooq and Bradshaw could be seen drinking beer and playing cards backstage before unleashing their own type of stiff punishment on competitors inside the ring. Three-time tag champs and one of the top teams of this or any other era.

SHANE MCMAHON

He might be the owner's son, but damn, Shane McMahon was also one of the most fearless performers of the era. He jumped from rafters, was thrown through glass, and even battled his father in a Street Fight at *WrestleMania X-Seven*.

ATTITUDE'S DEFINING MOMENTS: A TIMELINE

| JUNE 1996 | JULY 1996 | AUGUST 1996 | SEPTEMBER 1996 | OCTOBER 1996 |

JUNE 23, 1996

"AUSTIN 3:16 SAYS I JUST WHIPPED YOUR ASS"

Chris Jericho: "It's funny because you can't forget that moment. I think it's one of those things, like where you were when John Lennon was shot ... everybody remembers where they were. It's almost like the Texas Rattlesnake shed his skin that day. As if all the things that were holding him back just kind of exploded into a puff of dust on that day, because that was when Stone Cold Steve Austin was born. Has there ever been a more iconic catch phrase in the history of the business than Austin 3:16? I don't think so. I still see people wearing Austin 3:16 shirts to this day."

FEBRUARY 8, 1997

UNDERTAKER TOMBSTONES TRIPLE H AT PENN STATION

Booker T: "The Undertaker Tombstoned Triple H down an escalator! Let me just tell you this, kids: don't try this at home!"

| NOVEMBER 1996 | DECEMBER 1996 | JANUARY 1997 | FEBRUARY 1997 | MARCH 1997 |

FEBRUARY 24, 1997

ECW INVADES *RAW*

Paul Heyman: "ECW was always about the character— you cared about the characters. It wasn't about the fact that we did barbed wire matches for the sake of doing barbed wire matches. We put characters that you cared about into competing story lines, and it escalated to the point that you did a barbed wire or a cage match, or an extreme rules death match. It was never about the violence. And it's something that history has rewritten about ECW. We weren't the most violent promotion; we really weren't. WWE and WCW were doing stuff that was really crazier than we were."

AUGUST 18, 1997

THE ROCK JOINS THE NATION OF DOMINATION

D-Lo Brown: "Rocky had the poofy hair, which he hated, but he had hurt his knee, so they decided to put him with us when he came back. They realized what they were getting with Rocky. He really started to blossom within the concept of The Nation, and he was such a cool character—so much different than poofy-hair Rocky, and he really started to hit his stride. The great thing about The Nation was, since we were down at the bottom of the card, we could do a lot of trial and error. If we made a mistake early on, it wasn't a glaring mistake, so we could experiment on a nightly basis, and Rocky just continued to tweak his stuff depending on how the crowd reacted."

| APRIL 1997 | MAY 1997 | JUNE 1997 | JULY 1997 | AUGUST 1997 |

SEPTEMBER 22, 1997

STONE COLD STUNS MR. MCMAHON FOR FIRST TIME

Zack Ryder: "When Austin Stunned McMahon for the first time, he instantly became a WWE Legend."

174

OCTOBER 5, 1997

KANE DEBUTS

Kane: "I think the WWE Universe was so easily attracted to Kane because the Undertaker-Kane storyline was one of the best bits of storytelling WWE has ever done, and Paul Bearer was planting seeds about Kane for months before you ever actually saw me come up onscreen. You had this emotional, visceral reaction from Undertaker, which we'd never had before. I mean, who in the world could get into Undertaker's head, right?"

NOVEMBER 9, 1997

MONTREAL SCREWJOB: *SURVIVOR SERIES*

Daniel Bryan: "The Montreal Screwjob really made me hate Vince McMahon, because I loved Bret Hart. And just the idea that Bret got screwed and that Vince was the one who did it. It just made me think, 'God, gosh, this guy is such a … I would never want to work for this guy.'"

SEPTEMBER 1997 | OCTOBER 1997 | NOVEMBER 1997 | DECEMBER 1997 | JANUARY1998

OCTOBER 13, 1997

D-X FORMS: *RAW*

Shawn Michaels: "You can't get much more in your face than telling someone to 'Suck It' and then pointing to your crotch."

DECEMBER 15, 1997

STONE COLD THROWS THE ROCK'S INTERCONTINENTAL TITLE OFF A BRIDGE

John Cena: "In my mind, Stone Cold Steve Austin was the Attitude Era. Not because of Shock TV or anything like that; Steve was just one of those guys that had the attitude that carried the era. He spoke exactly how he felt. If he was pissed off at you, he would let you know. If he liked you, he'd let you know. If he was going to whip your ass, he'd let you know, and then whip your ass. There's been nobody like him, and he defined that era in the WWE timeline."

MIKE TYSON MEETS STONE COLD STEVE AUSTIN

Stone Cold Steve Austin: "When Tyson pushed me, for some reason just a ton of hundred-dollar bills started flying out of his pockets. His guys are looking around the ring and hundred-dollar bills are flying everywhere, so as his guys are trying to scoop up the money, I'm over here kicking, clawing, and scratching trying to get that son of bitch, and the people are going ape shit. I'll tell you what, if they would have put Mike Tyson vs. Stone Cold on a pay-per-view, I don't think anybody would have beaten it to this day."

| FEBRUARY 1998 | MARCH 1998 | APRIL 1998 | MAY 1998 |

MARCH 30, 1998

TRIPLE H REFORMS DX, X-PAC'S RETURN: *RAW*

X-Pac: "So I'm at home with a broken neck. I had successful surgery. Ten months I was out. And I'm getting paid—full pay the whole time, you know, everything taken care of. And right before I'm ready to come back, Eric (Bischoff) gets pissed at Kevin (Nash) and Scott (Hall). And their contracts were so iron-clad and they had all their bases covered, like it was very difficult for them to be punished in any way. So for Eric to get to them, he punished me and basically fired me by FedEx to try to put those guys in line. And it didn't work very well for Eric. He'll admit it was one of the biggest mistakes he ever made."

APRIL 27, 1998

D-X INVADES *NITRO*

X-Pac: "I just always wonder what would have happened if we would have made it into the building. You know, what would the (WCW) boys have done?"

JUNE 28, 1998
UNDERTAKER VS. MANKIND: HELL IN A CELL

Dolph Ziggler:

"Mankind flew off the Cell. That was one of the coolest things I have ever seen. It looked like he fell fifty feet through a table, onto the ground, and I honestly couldn't believe it had just happened before my eyes."

JULY 26, 1998
SABLE'S HANDPRINT BIKINI

Kofi Kingston: "Man, Sable, was one of the hottest, if not *the* hottest Diva of all time. I remember being in middle school, and you know, drooling over her like so many people were. And then when she took her top off, I think I, along with all my friends and a lot of kids around the nation, wanted to see what was underneath her garments. And sure enough, she had the handprints there. I mean, you talk about risqué, me and my friends were definitely, definitely amused."

JUNE 1998		JULY 1998		AUGUST 1998		SEPTEMBER 1998

JUNE 29, 1998
BRAWL FOR ALL TOURNAMENT BEGINS

X-Pac: "If there was anything in the Attitude Era that I thought was a terrible concept, it was the Brawl for All. It was when they had a bunch of us—not us as in me, because I wouldn't have done it—but, you know, they had our guys out there with boxing gloves on, fighting each other. Guys were getting hurt and what was it to prove? I just thought that was a really stupid thing."

AUGUST 3, 1998
KAIENTAI TRIES TO "CHOPPY-CHOPPY" THE "PEE PEE" OFF VAL VENIS

Dolph Ziggler: "Kaientai actually kidnapped Val Venis and they were going to chop off his most important part. And somehow, somehow, the lights went out. We didn't know what happened. I was at the edge of my seat until the following week, and we found out that John Wayne Bobbitt had actually come in and saved the day. He saved Val Venis … and little Val."

SEPTEMBER 28, 1998
STONE COLD'S ZAMBONI

Daniel Bryan: "The thing that I remember most about Austin driving the Zamboni … it was just chaos. And it's been played so much that it's ingrained in your head. I can still see it in my brain, as he's driving down there, and the spraying and everything—it was fantastic."

OCTOBER 16, 1998
BANG: 3:16 SAYS VINCE JUST PISSED HIS PANTS

The Miz: "Austin is great at beating up his boss and making Vince McMahon just pay for everything he has ever done. And I think all the WWE Universe, all the WWE fans, really embraced Austin because of it. Because we all know what a bad boss is like. And we all want to do it to our boss. So when Austin put a gun up to Vince's head, and Vince starts wetting himself, and Austin shoots, and it says 'Bang,' I think everyone was just at peace and at ease. Because we all wished we could do it to our boss."

`OCTOBER 1998`

`NOVEMBER 1998`

OCTOBER 5, 1998
STONE COLD ATTACKS VINCE MCMAHON IN HOSPITAL

CM Punk: "Not only do you have Vince McMahon, the boss that everybody hates, laid up in a hospital—ha-ha, the boss is hurt—you also have Mick Foley being incredibly annoying, but entertaining and funny at the same time, trying to cheer him up. That's where Socko was born! Right? He had Clownie, I think he busted out the Socko, and then of course Stone Cold Steve Austin cracked the boss in the head with a bedpan and beat him up in the hospital. Classic."

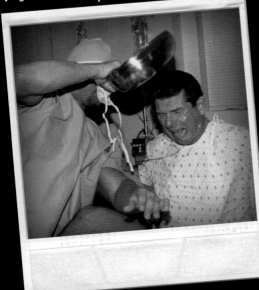

OCTOBER 12, 1998
STONE COLD FILLS MR. MCMAHON'S CORVETTE WITH CEMENT: *RAW*

Daniel Bryan: "When Austin poured concrete into Vince's Corvette, I thought, 'Man, that's a lot of money.'"

NOVEMBER 15, 1998

THE ROCK CROWNED CORPORATE CHAMPION

Stone Cold Steve Austin: "I remember as Rock and Nation of Domination kept going on and on, Rock started getting a lot of momentum as a babyface. He was getting a positive reaction from the fans because he was so entertaining. He was so electrifying. He was so energetic in the way he did things, you couldn't help but like him. So, they go to Survivor Series '98, him and Mick Foley. Then Shane and Vince screwed Mick Foley, but Rock aligns himself with Vince McMahon and becomes Corporate Champion. Man, I knew right then that our paths were going to cross. And they would cross several months down the road, it was absolutely brilliant."

DECEMBER 1998

NOVEMBER 19, 1998

HELL'S HENCHMEN INTRODUCED (LATER KNOWN AS THE ACOLYTES/APA)

Ron Simmons: "There will never be another tag team like APA. When you find someone that you can love like a brother, like I love him (Bradshaw), and we respect each other and get along so well outside the ring, it's just a magical thing. People can feel and pick that up. We weren't turning things on just for the camera. Just like The Nation, we were off-screen best pals. We would talk about things outside of wrestling. This was one of the times I had in wrestling where I knew we'd never be able to top what we were doing. Next to being world champion, being in APA is right there next to that. It's a time I always cherished and always will. There will never be another tag team to top what we had. The people didn't care if we were heels or fan favorites. They just saw us going out there and kicking ass and entertaining."

MICK FOLEY WINS WWE CHAMPIONSHIP

Mick Foley: "I'd love to talk about Tony Schiavone giving away the results. I watched the replay of *Nitro*, and they were having a particularly bad show … even though it was from the Georgia Dome, live. And when I heard the words, there's no reason to turn the channel—Mick Foley, or Mankind, who wrestled here as WCW's Cactus Jack, wins their world title, and he said, 'Wow, that will put a lot of butts in seats' … It just took a special night, it sucked the joy out of it for me, and it really hurt me because I had really extended myself during my time at WCW. I was never someone who made the really big money, and I thought, if anything, those guys should be kind of happy for me. I mean, I was a pretty good guy, a hardworking employee, and they took away the fun for me on that night."

MR. MCMAHON WINS ROYAL RUMBLE

Seth Rollins: "Yeah, Mr. McMahon winning the Royal Rumble, it really put a stamp on how in control Vince was. He had everyone under his thumb. And the fact that he was able to win a Royal Rumble at his age and his lack of experience in the ring just proved that you couldn't ever doubt Vince McMahon or The Corporation."

JANUARY 1999   FEBRUARY 1999   MARCH 1999

FEBRUARY 14, 1999

BIG SHOW'S DEBUT

Big Show: "When I was interjected in the middle of the Austin-McMahon rivalry, it was my first experience, really, with a large, mainstream thought-out angle. You had Steve Austin who was over like nobody I had ever seen before. His popularity and the relationship that he had with the fans was so different from anything I had ever experienced before. I mean, there were fans before that liked certain guys, and those guys were very black or white, good or bad. But Austin did everything like a bad guy. He flipped people off, he drank beer. He pretty much did whatever he wanted to. But he symbolized everybody that had worked for a tyrant, to rise up against that tyrant, and Vince was the ultimate tyrant. He owned the company. He owned everything. He owned your soul, you know? Austin was your red-blooded American that shoved it right up his nose, it was good."

MARCH 7, 1999

KURT ANGLE DEBUTS

Edge: "Kurt was a great foil and vice versa—we played off each other great. Had a great connection in the ring, always did. From day one, our first match was like, 'Boom, we've got something here.' Kurt has that ability with a lot of people. It's a testament to how good he is."

MARCH 22, 1999

STONE COLD GIVES CORPORATION A BEER BATH

Dolph Ziggler:
"When Austin sprayed beer all over everybody and Vince McMahon, I thought that was one of the coolest things in the world. I'm a huge Austin fan, and I love the fact that he sprayed his boss, soaking him with beer. He fell all over the place—it was really cool."

APRIL 12, 1999

THE ROCK THROWS STONE COLD OFF BRIDGE

The Rock: "The chemistry between myself and Stone Cold Steve Austin was—and is—very, very special and unique, and we knew that we had something that was intangible. That was an X-factor when we first started doing our thing."

APRIL 1999   MAY 1999   JUNE 1999

APRIL 26, 1999

UNDERTAKER KIDNAPS STEPHANIE MCMAHON: *BACKLASH 1999, RAW*

Booker T:
"The Undertaker's Unholy Wedding— that was a sight to see, in more than one way. There was Stephanie, hung out to dry like a big pair of drawers on a clothesline just flapping in the breeze."

APRIL 29, 1999

CORPORATE MINISTRY FORMS: *SMACKDOWN*

Tyson Kidd: "That was like a Royal Rumble's worth of guys in that group alone. It felt like there were 20 or 30 guys, and for me, watching it, I was already wrestling at the time, so I was watching and I was like, 'How can anyone really beat these guys?' There were 30 of them and they were main guys. They didn't have Austin but they had basically everybody else."

JUNE 7, 1999
THE HIGHER POWER REVEALED: *RAW*

Vince McMahon: "I think a lot of people say, 'Okay, um, what's Vince really like? Is he like the guy on television? Is he like that way in the corporate life? How close are the two?'… So I'm wondering myself now, which is the character and which is me. I guess maybe it's a blend, you know, and I would suggest that one is exaggerated a little bit, but I'm not so sure which one. In other words, I'm not going to tell you, how's that?"

JULY 22, 1999
EDGE WINS FIRST SINGLES CHAMPIONSHIP

Edge: "At one point, I heard it was tossed around that I was going to be a deaf mute, because they didn't think that I could talk. Man, talk about the kiss of death in wrestling. I knew I could. I knew I could. I was nervous, but that's why I went to school for radio. That's why I was getting all this experience. You know, I didn't bring all of that to the table with me. I knew it was there, and I had done it, but I didn't know what they wanted. So I pulled back, and I thought, 'Okay, I think they just want me to be me,' and in doing that, they thought maybe I should be a deaf mute. Doesn't say a lot for my personality, does it?"

JULY 1999

AUGUST 1999

JULY 5, 1999
THE HARDY BOYZ CAPTURE FIRST TAG TEAM TITLE

Matt Hardy: "We were on the ramp and I was looking over at everyone. We were the tag team champions. Matt and Jeff Hardy, two kids from Cameron, North Carolina—what kind of odds would you really give them?—were the representation of the best tag team in the wrestling business. We were holding tag team titles that every legendary tag team before us had held. It was really such a quick moment, but all these thoughts were going through my head about the sacrifices we'd made. And, wow, this is a real living, breathing example of 'dreams do come true.' It was overwhelming, more than anything else. The hugs between me, Jeff, and Michael Hayes were as real as they could get. Sometimes things in the sports-entertainment business are manufactured … nothing about that moment was manufactured."

AUGUST 9, 1999
Y2J COUNTDOWN HITS ZERO, CHRIS JERICHO DEBUTS: *RAW*

The Rock: "Chris Jericho was a great free agent, if you will, coming over from WCW. He made one of the most memorable entrances in the history of the WWE when he came out and interrupted me. That was a great launching point for him, and it was a great launching point for us, too… we knew we had something pretty cool and we were gonna do some special things down the road, and we did."

AUGUST 26, 1999

SMACKDOWN DEBUTS ON UPN

Stephanie McMahon: "*SmackDown* was The Rock's show. I actually think that Rock branded *SmackDown* and 'smackdown' became an actual word in the Urban Dictionary. Now it's used all the time by every media outlet, every time you turn around. But *SmackDown* was just that. It was on a broadcast platform, had the ability to reach families, and *SmackDown* has always been PG. It was a huge momentum turner for us."

SEPTEMBER 16, 1999

MR. MCMAHON WINS WWE CHAMPIONSHIP

Chris Jericho: "Vince fancies himself a wrestler, like deep down inside he thinks that he's really good but he's really bad. He's a great performer facially and knowing where to be; his timing is great, but his actual athleticism is atrocious. He reminds me a lot of a crazy gazelle that's been driven insane getting bitten by bees or something."

SEPTEMBER 1999

OCTOBER 1999

SEPTEMBER 9, 1999

JEFF JARRETT HITS FABULOUS MOOLAH WITH GUITAR, LOCKS MAE YOUNG IN FIGURE FOUR

Dolph Ziggler:
"Mae Young and Moolah were two of the toughest broads in the entire world. And if you think Mae Young getting Powerbombed off the stage is something, Moolah took Jeff Jarrett's guitar; it got blasted over her face and disintegrated in Jeff Jarrett's hands."

SEPTEMBER 27, 1999

THIS IS YOUR LIFE, ROCK: *RAW*

Triple H: "This is Your Life with Foley and Rock was an unforgettable moment. Unforgettable for me, because it was like eighteen minutes long, and I was underneath the stage, bent over for the entire time, screaming at them to finish. I was like a cripple coming out from under the stage."

OCTOBER 17, 1999

CHYNA BECOMES FIRST (AND ONLY) FEMALE TO WIN INTERCONTINENTAL CHAMPIONSHIP

Pete Gas: "The fact that Chyna won the title is attributed to how hard she worked. She didn't have the easiest time coming through WWE. She was teased and given a hard time about her looks and how masculine she was, but Chyna was such a sweetheart. I remember working out with her one time. She had I were doing this leg workout that was so intense, I couldn't even believe I was able to walk out of the gym. Her work ethic was amazing, and she wrestled as good as the guys. She really was The Ninth Wonder of the World."

NOVEMBER 11, 1999

BIG BOSS MAN CRASHES BIG SHOW'S FATHER'S FUNERAL: *SMACKDOWN*

Jerry Lawler: "I think one of the most outrageous things that I ever witnessed was when the Boss Man just completely destroyed the funeral services of Big Show's father. It was like a funeral turned into a wedding. You know, at a wedding you see the car, and the bride and groom drive away with a bunch of cans hanging off the back of the car. Well, the Boss Man was driving away with a coffin dragging behind his car!"

NOVEMBER 1999   DECEMBER 1999   JANUARY 2000

NOVEMBER 29, 1999

TRIPLE H MARRIES STEPHANIE MCMAHON: *RAW*

John Cena: "I was there. I was there for that. In the crowd, as a fan. It was awesome. Huge, big time wedding. It went off almost without a hitch, and then bam! It's like watching a video excerpt from *The Hangover*, it was a really, really cool deal."

JANUARY 13, 2000

MANKIND MORPHS INTO CACTUS JACK: *SMACKDOWN*

The Miz: "Mick Foley has created four different characters. You have Mick Foley who is a bestselling author, loving father; and then you have Cactus Jack, hardcore; Mankind, crazy; and then you have Dude Love, the ladies' man. Some people can't get one character for an audience reaction. Mick has gotten four, and not only that, but during the Monday Night War, you get to see three of the four; you get to see Mankind, Cactus Jack, and Dude Love all do a promo together. So it was interesting to see WWE as well as Mick Foley able to do a cool, interesting promo that no one ever thought they would see because we all know that Mick Foley is all three of those guys."

THE RADICALZ APPEAR AS BACKSTAGE GUESTS OF MICK FOLEY

Eddie Guerrero: "WWE had the momentum already (in the Monday Night Wars), but we were the nail in the coffin."

FEBRUARY 2000   MARCH 2000

FEBRUARY 28, 2000

MAE YOUNG GIVES BIRTH TO A HAND

Mark Henry: "Mae Young was awesome. Out of all the people I've worked with in the 18 years I've been in the business, she's the most fearless. Nothing rattled her. There will never be another woman like her in wrestling. People all the time come up to me and ask, 'Hey, how's your son The Hand?' I'm like, 'He's fine.' It happens all the time. I'm happy with the fact that some things that I did will never die. Memories like the hand will outlive all of us."

MARCH 2, 2000

HARDCORE TITLE DEFENDED 24/7: CRASH HOLLY

The Miz: "I loved the 24/7 Hardcore Championship. I always wanted to do that in the WWE, where the title is open 24/7, because I remember them going in a playground. Now I can totally see people backstage going, 'How can they do this?' This is opening up the business and blah blah. That to me was so entertaining, and it still sticks in my mind that they were at, I think, Mall of America, and they were going down slides, going down, and I mean it was entertaining. I think Molly Holly actually had it for one second because she pinned Hurricane. So I remember Crash Holly being that Hardcore Champion with the 24/7 rule, and it just made for great entertaining television."

MARCH 13, 2000

BUBBA RAY DUDLEY POWERBOMBS MAE YOUNG THROUGH A TABLE

Kofi Kingston: "How are you going to Powerbomb Mae Young? Come on, now! Off the stage? It was one of those things; you saw it happening, and you didn't quite think it was going to happen. And sure enough, being the bad boys that the Dudleyz were, they Powerbombed poor, innocent Mae Young through a table, off the stage. Those are some bad boys."

APRIL 27, 2000

STONE COLD STEVE AUSTIN BLOWS UP THE DX BUS

The Miz:
"Stone Cold Steve Austin is always known for destruction, but I think the best destruction that he has ever done was blowing up D-Generation X's bus. Fantastic."

APRIL 2000	MAY 2000	JUNE 2000

MARCH 19, 2000

TRISH STRATUS DEBUTS

Natalya: "Trish Stratus will go down as not only one of the best Divas in the history of WWE, but one of my personal favorites. Being that she's Canadian, I'm always a little partial to my fellow Canadians. But Trish, I think she really reinvented the term 'Diva.' And she was kind of one of the forerunners in establishing what are known today as Divas. Not just women in wrestling, but what we do now is extraordinary. There's nothing that we can't do, and Trish really embodied that. Whether it was being able to speak, whether it was being able to perform in the ring, whether it was being able to slap Mr. McMahon, which both of us have done … she can do it all. I think she just brought that sparkle and energy, and people could feel it. She didn't have to say a word; people could just connect with her. She was bold, bright, and beautiful, and she'll never be replaced."

JUNE 5, 2000

RIKISHI DELIVERS STINKFACE TO TRISH

Rikishi: "The Stinkface was actually a hold by the gentleman named Ray Traylor (Big Boss Man). We actually wrestled in Mobile, Alabama. I happened to give Ray Traylor a clothesline in the corner, and when Ray Traylor dropped, I didn't see him drop in the corner. And I can hear this one old lady—I was looking at her—I could hear this one old lady saying, 'Rikishi! Stick your butt in his face!' I said, 'What?' She said, 'Stick your butt in his face!'"

AUGUST 27, 2000

SHANE MCMAHON AND STEVE BLACKMON FALL FROM THE TOP OF THE ENTRANCE STAGE

Pete Gas: "Growing up, Shane has always been fearless. Everything he does, he wants to make it bigger than life. I remember we were in Boston and I didn't want to watch the action on a monitor; I wanted to watch it live, so I snuck out into the arena. I had a perfect angle to watch it, and I was so amazed by what Shane was willing to do for his family's company. He put his whole life on the line and he just didn't care. He's always been a daredevil, but this topped them all."

JULY 2000   AUGUST 2000   SEPTEMBER 2000

SEPTEMBER 21, 2000

KURT ANGLE KISSES STEPHANIE MCMAHON

Kurt Angle: "The McMahons on TV and the McMahon family in real life are very different. Linda and Stephanie are two of the most loving people I've ever met. Shane McMahon is a ... actually he's not much different than he is on TV. He's kind of crazy, very energetic, likes to joke around. But when it comes to business, he's very serious, too. I never met a more caring family. They have the reality show *Hogan Knows Best*, and it's a pretty cool show. You know, I watch it and I respect the heck out of Hulk Hogan. But I would much rather watch *McMahon Knows Best*. To see them in real life and to see them as characters on TV, that would be the most intriguing thing to watch. I can't imagine a day in the life of Vince McMahon and his family, because there is probably no soap opera that could match it."

187

DECEMBER 12, 2000
RIKISHI'S FALL FROM HELL

Rikishi: "You know, there was so much hype around that whole Hell in a Cell. Sitting in the locker room, I wanted to do my part, as far as, 'What can I do to be a part of something that's already great, to make it greater? For me to carry my load?' And we came up with the deal ... you know, 'Taker has this saying, 'I'll make you famous.' Cactus Jack did the deal where he threw him off, onto the announcer's table. So, when we talked about that bump there, I'll tell you, man, I was a nervous wreck. I didn't know if I could pull it off. I didn't know what would happen. Because, that was a pretty high place for me to take a bump off of. And, you know, it's one of those things, we're up there during the heat of the moment, 18,000 people screaming their heads off."

OCTOBER 2000

NOVEMBER 2000

DECEMBER 2000

MARCH 26, 2001

WWE PURCHASES WCW

Vince McMahon: "I would have preferred to have not gone through the Monday Night War. I know the old adage, 'what doesn't kill you makes you stronger.' Generally speaking, I would agree with that. But there were some rotten times when you're David competing with Goliath. You have to think differently. I think that you need to come up with guerilla tactics; you need to find a way to compete with people, and you don't have to compete with them the way they want you to compete. If you're fighting with a giant, you have to be careful; you can't go toe to toe because you'll get knocked down. And there were times when we got knocked down and almost out."

JANUARY 2001	FEBRUARY 2001	MARCH 2001	APRIL 2001

APRIL 1, 2001

WRESTLEMANIA X-7 GOES DOWN AS ARGUABLY THE GREATEST *WRESTLEMANIA* OF ALL TIME

David Otunga: "When Edge speared Jeff off the ladder, it was unbelievable. Edge climbs up the ladder, now Jeff's hanging from the title, and I'm thinking, 'Okay, what's he going to do here?' And of all things, he spears him from the ladder! Hits him in midair. They fall what had to be 15 to 20 feet. Unbelievable."

THE END OF AN ERA

"It was highly successful at the time.
It was what the people wanted."

—Vince McMahon

"... How far can you go when you're competing like we were head-to-head with Turner? It was almost like you had to bring out the kitchen sink."

—Vince McMahon

According to Vince McMahon, once WWE bought WCW, the need for shock power and attention-grabbing—even death defying—stunts was over. It was time to bring the Attitude Era to an end.

"It was highly successful at the time. It was what the people wanted," says McMahon. "And then, as time goes on, you again morph and change, and give the audience what they want. [They] said they'd had enough of the Attitude Era.

"And how far can you go when you're competing like we were head-to-head with Turner? It was almost like you had to bring out the kitchen sink. What was going to be next, you know, an armored car? A tank? What are you going to do next? And we knew they were going to burn out because they did what we call 'hot-shotting' all the time. Give people all kinds of crazy matches and things of that nature. I sort of liken it back to Jake 'The Snake' Roberts when he was a performer for us. You had to use Jake sparingly because, if you used Jake every week, he'd pull out this python or whatever snake it was and, you know, 'Oh there's the snake again…' You become jaded. If you used him on occasion, it was like, 'Oh my God! There's a snake on the loose in the ring!'"

WrestleMania X-7 serves as the poetic last page in the Attitude Era chapter, wrapping up the storyline and rivalry between The Rock and Stone Cold. Steve Austin won the WWE Championship thanks to interference from his Attitude Era nemesis, Vince McMahon—not to mention his stunning assault on The Great One.

With McMahon and Austin toasting each other in the middle of the ring, the pay-per-view (and era) had come to a close. "I never thought I'd be toasting McMahon, but I've always loved to play the villain, and it was a great way to close out the era," says Stone Cold Steve Austin.

And while some argue that the era truly ended when WWE bought WCW, or later, during the WCW/ECW invasion, stars like Austin see *WrestleMania X-7* as the historic last ride, thanks in part to the significance of the show's ending. The era that kicked off with Austin 3:16 just kicked fans in the hearts with Austin and McMahon finally working as one.

"Hell, it was an interesting storyline, and I had my greatest run working as a babyface," adds Austin, "but working heel, that's what I love. And joining Vince gave me the perfect opportunity to make that turn."

With the Attitude Era now over, it was time to reignite the brand and introduce a set of new stars and personas. To do this, Vince McMahon stood up in the WWE locker room and asked who was ready to lead the next generation. Ruthless Aggression was about to begin, and McMahon tabbed John Cena as the man to lead his company into this new era.

"Who is ready to step up and try to get the brass ring? Is there anyone here who has the balls enough to go do this? And Cena raised his hand and said, 'I do.'"

—Vince McMahon

TED TURNER'S FEELINGS ON THE ATTITUDE ERA

Remembers McMahon: "Ted (Turner), when he began to lose in the television ratings, our paths crossed," remembers McMahon, "and Ted said, 'Well, the only reason you're winning right now, Vince, is because you show more of the tit.' I said, 'What?!' And it was like, 'Yeah, your product is more salacious than mine. That's why you're winning.' 'Ted, we entertain people.' For him to even say something like that told me a lot about who Ted Turner was or how he looked at our business. It was just, like, so lowlife, unbelievable, sexist, and everything else, you know? Nonetheless, that was his philosophy and his view, I think, of the quote 'wrasslin' business.'"

"Now we give the audience what they want in a far more sophisticated way."

—Vince McMahon

"That's always been a part of who Vince McMahon is: ruthless and very aggressive. And it stemmed from a meeting that we had about a week earlier with all of the WWE talent. I didn't see anyone there with that kind of oomph," says McMahon. "Who is ready to step up and try to get the brass ring? Is there anyone here who has the balls enough to go do this? And Cena raised his hand and said, 'I do.' Two others did as well, so I interviewed all of them afterward, but John was the only one who meant it. So the following week, John Cena exemplified ruthless aggression and did a really good job of it.

"As I recall, it was a situation where John was really, really pumped. He knew the opportunity, was going to seize the opportunity and not let it go. Kurt Angle, our Olympian, was a tremendous performer; for John Cena to come out, this kid with all this ruthless aggression, and challenge Kurt Angle, that said something about John Cena."

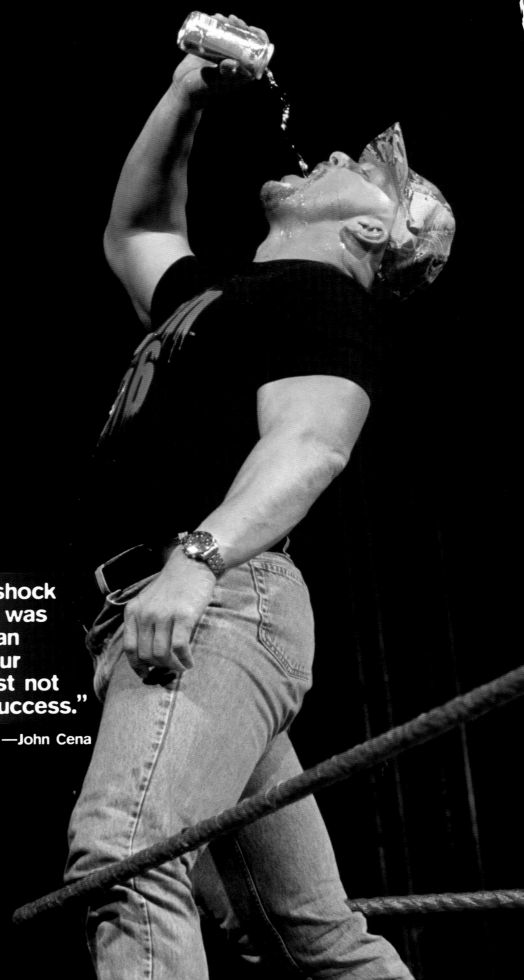

And that challenge, that aggression, is what bridged the gap between Attitude and today's far more scripted PG era. "To reach a much broader audience, we had to go for the jugular, so to speak, back in the Attitude Era. We had no choice competing with Turner," says McMahon. "You had to do something like that. Now we don't have to. Now we give the audience what they want in a far more sophisticated way."

But that doesn't mean the performers and fans don't miss the occasional beer bath. Adds Austin: "The Attitude Era was one of the best times of my life. It was an awesome time, a very special time, and I don't think we'll ever see anything like it in sports-entertainment again."

"It was shock TV, but shock TV only goes so far. It was just about, hey, what can we do next to shock our audience? But that's just not the way to long-term success."

—John Cena

JOHN CENA ON WHY THE ATTITUDE ERA HAD TO END

"It was shock TV, but shock TV only goes so far. It was just about, hey, what can we do next to shock our audience? But that's just not the way to long-term success. The WCW versus WWE competition scenario is what truly fueled the ratings. And internally, when you're faced with competition, it forces you to do your best. Back then, there was a group of people who really wanted to defeat WCW, but the content is not something I hold close. Now, there is no external competition; the competition comes from within and it's just a different time. I hate to talk about one era versus another era. To me, it's just all WWE."

"Now, there is no external competition; the competition comes from within and it's just a different time. I hate to talk about one era versus another era. To me, it's just all WWE."

—John Cena

ONE FOR THE ROAD

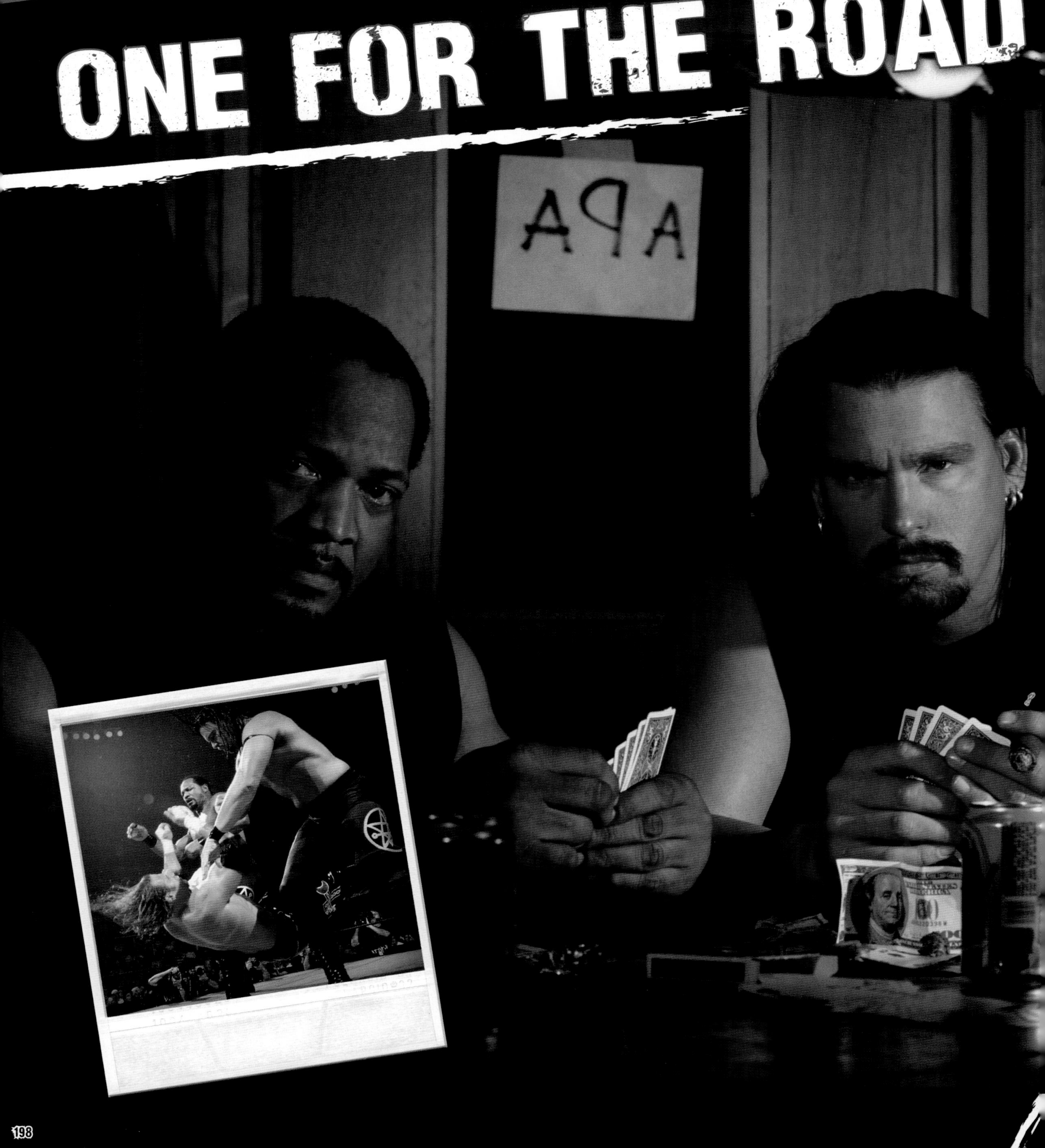

Traveling up to 300 days a year, Attitude Era Superstars were as comfortable inside a rental car or an airplane as they were inside the ring.

Take a roster featuring the likes of DX, Val Venis, and The Nation, and you never know what type of trouble they'll find. These are their stories.

Ron Simmons: "JBL, myself, and Teddy Long were traveling together, and John and I had celebrated that night because we had won the Tag Team Championship. We were drinking that night, so Teddy had to drive us to the next show. We were half hungover, and we had been drinking so much that we were giving Teddy a hard time the entire trip. He couldn't even think we were razzing him so much. And before you know it, he's up to like 85 miles per hour. He's speeding and we're continuing to give him hell, so he hits the gas and goes faster. Next thing you know, there's a cop behind us and we're getting pulled over. The cop comes up and leans into the window and says, 'Do you know how fast you were going? Do I smell alcohol?' So I blurt out, 'What are you now, a bloodhound?' This really angered the state trooper, so he goes, 'Who has been drinking?' So I yell, 'Me!' and John says, 'Me too!' And then the trooper looks at Teddy and he's pleading like, 'Not me officer, I haven't been drinking.' The trooper tells Teddy to get out of the car and gives him a sobriety test, which he passed. But then he gives Teddy a ticket. John and I offer to pay the ticket for him, but then once we're back on the road, we start giving him hell again. We were supposed to be going from one city in Kentucky to a different city in Kentucky, and it really wasn't supposed to be a long drive, but then two hours later, we're still in the car. We're like, 'What the hell is going on here?' Damn it, he was so distracted by everything we were doing in the car and all the trash we were talking that he ended up headed toward Michigan. He was so frustrated and so mad, he couldn't think straight. He ended up making us late for the next show."

"It's about 6 p.m. when Snoop shows up, and within ten minutes of him closing the door to his locker room, the entire area smelled like the strongest weed you could ever smell in your life."

—D-Lo Brown

D-Lo Brown: "We were doing a show in Chicago at the Rosemont Horizon, and Jesse Ventura was going to be there. This is when he was the governor of Minnesota. At the same time, Snoop Dogg came in. In the bowels of the arena, it's really small back there and all of the locker rooms are close together. It's about 6 p.m. when Snoop shows up, and within ten minutes of him closing the door to his locker room, the entire area smelled like the strongest weed you could ever smell in your life. Ten minutes later, Snoop comes out all glassy eyed and he's talking to everybody. In the next locker room over, there's Jesse Ventura and he has Secret Service agents manning the door. We were all looking at this like, man, this is not going to end well. Fortunately, everything turned out cool. I guess as long as the Secret Service kept the governor safe, they didn't care what Snoop was smoking."

Ron Simmons: "My character, being Farooq, dressed up in a Muslim fashion. I remember this one time I was in Chicago and we were getting ready to do a show at the Rosemont Pavilion. I had no idea that there was a Muslim convention at the Hyatt we were staying at. So I was running a little late for the show and I had my Nation ring gear already on, complete with the hat, when I came downstairs. As I'm racing through the lobby, I get spotted by the guys doing the convention and they run up to me. They're like, 'Oh my god, it's Farooq. We listen to you all the time. Your messages are right on point, and you stand for everything the Islamic Nation stands for.' I didn't want to tell them this really wasn't what I was standing for, but I didn't want to break character either. So they say, 'Look, we're getting ready to go to the convention center right now and we'd love for you to be the guest speaker.' I'm like, Holy crap! I said, 'Well look, I'm running late for a show right now.' I didn't want to be disrespectful, but I didn't want them to think I stood for their principles. I thought about it, and I figured if I told them this was all an act and I was just going through the motions, I didn't think it would sit too well with these guys, so I decided to go in and do the speech. I gave a two- or three-minute speech based off what I used to say on *Raw*, and I couldn't believe it. They gave me a standing ovation. That's when I really knew The Nation was starting to take off. All of a sudden I was getting flooded with letters from all over the world. It got to the point where what I was saying really, really serious for a lot of people. I got a lot of heartfelt letters like, man, we've been waiting for someone like you to come along and speak up for us and give us a voice. It got really serious; it got really intense, and I even started getting letters from prisoners. It was unbelievable."

Mark Henry: The Rock was so high maintenance with his Rocky Maivia poofy hair that he was always making us late. We used to live together, and I'd be like, 'C'mon, man, we have to go!' And he'd be standing there still doing his hair 15 minutes later. One time, I was like, 'I'm out,' and I just left him there with his poofy hair. He called me up when I got to the show and begged me to come back and get him. It was too funny. We used to argue like brothers, and we still talk today. It's funny, though, because a lot of what we did on the road not only helped with The Nation's chemistry in the ring, but some of it even ended up on air. I remember when The Rock, D-Lo, and myself were in the car and we were listening to Dr. Dre's *The Chronic*. Dr. Dre said something like, 'It's time to lay the smackdown,' and The Rock thought it was funny. So any time we were traveling and he wanted something, he'd be like, 'If we don't eat something soon, I'm going to lay the smackdown.' Then he started saying it on TV, and then it evolved into 'I'm going to lay the smackdown on your candy ass.' Before you knew it, the TV show *Velocity* even changed its name to *SmackDown*. It just shows the influence of The Nation to this day."

"The Rock was so high maintenance with his Rocky Maivia poofy hair that he was always making us late. We used to live together, and I'd be like, 'C'mon, man, we have to go!' And he'd be standing there still doing his hair 15 minutes later."

—Mark Henry

Triple H: "Big Show and I were on a flight on the company plane, which is like a 12-seater. We were going to a press conference for a pay-per-view. It's like an hour and a half flight, and this was our relationship: I blister Paul, and he takes it. He tries to fight back, but he's like an unarmed man. I tell him all the time, 'You're like clubbing a baby seal, it's just fun.' So I'm on him like this the whole flight. I think Bradshaw might have been on there too. Jericho was on there, and Vince was chiming in. We're blistering him the whole flight. At the end of the flight, Paul—when Paul gets really mad sometimes he stutters—started to get mad to where he started to stutter, which just increased the funniness factor by a hundred. The more he tried to defend himself, the more he would stutter. So we landed and finally taxi over to the gate and he can't wait to get off the plane. He's practically standing up, which is amusing also. Him standing up in the plane holding his little bag just waiting to get off. And then as soon as the door cracks open he's like, 'I'm out of here!'"

"He's mad and says something derogatory to me on his way through the door. And it's like you walk through the one door and turn and go down the stairs. Well, as he went through the door, he closed it back behind him. Then he obviously turned to walk out, but all of a sudden we're all laughing at him because he's so mad. Then, boom! The whole plane shook like we just hit something. I'm like, 'Oh my god.' I jump and slide the door open, and Paul is lying on the stairway of the plane. The railings are broken, one of the stairs is broken, and he's lying there in pain.

"It was slippery, and he had gone to lean on the railing of the plane and the railing broke. He went way up in the air and did a complete flip and landed on the jetway—after he had just been blistered for an hour and a half about being fat and all that stuff. He was so mad. We went to a press conference the next day, and I tell the story about how he fell down the stairs, and then he was doubly mad. It was The Giant mad at that point. I'm telling you he's an endless wealth of material."

Lita: "Trish and I went to the Alamo and our tour guide was really not impressed with us when we asked him where the basement was like in *Pee-Wee's Big Adventure*. We were the bane of his existence, like, 'How many times am I going to be asked where the basement is!' Granted, I'm sure it gets annoying, but it was like I just said, 'Your mother sucks!' It was like I ruined his day. We laughed so hard at his reaction. It was 11 a.m.— how did we already ruin this guy's day? It was fun, though, because when we first started out, we didn't take time to enjoy ourselves in all of these cities and countries we were able to travel to. But when we were able to stop and play tourist, we had a great time."

> **"We go outside to throw up in the bushes, but then Rodney gets the idea to throw up on the hood of our rental car to see whose throw-up would last longer on the hood as we drove."**
>
> **—Pete Gas**

Pete Gas: "When I started wrestling, I was 285 pounds and I wasn't in any type of good shape at all. When you're around all the guys who are so ripped and look the way they do, you feel obligated, you feel motivation to get yourself in better shape. So I was dieting at the time, and we were in Cleveland. We had stopped at a Denny's, but I felt bad for eating all of this junk. So I turn to Rodney and I'm like, 'I think I'm going to go throw this up.' Rodney is so competitive, whether we're in the gym, in the ring, or wherever. He always wanted to turn everything into a competition. So he says, 'You know what, I'll throw up with you.' We go outside to throw up in the bushes, but then Rodney gets the idea to throw up on the hood of our rental car to see whose throw-up would last longer on the hood as we drove. So we're stupid enough where I did it, Rodney did it, and then Joey Abs joins in and throws up with us. As we're puking on the car, out come Matt and Jeff Hardy, Edge and Christian, Val Venis, Test, and Prince Albert. Of course, Jeff sees something disgusting, and he instantly runs over to get a better look. Jeff was like, 'What are you guys doing?' So we explain how we didn't want to keep the food down and decided to throw up, but instead of being disgusted, Jeff sticks his finger in Joey Abs' throw-up and tastes it. This caused Christian to run to the bushes, and he starts puking his brains out over how disgusting Jeff was. Next thing you know, we hop in the car, and we're laughing so hard because as we're driving, you can see the piles of puke vibrating on the hood of the car. And before you know it, all three piles splatter across the windshield at the same time. Our car is completely covered in throw-up, and we're trying to use the windshield wipers, but all that does is push the throw-up to the side and it starts flying everywhere. We're dying laughing until we get pulled over by a cop. Rodney rolls the window down, and the cop is like, 'What the hell happened to your car?' I roll my window down and I'm like, 'Officer, you're not going to believe this, but we're wrestlers and we portray these bad guys, and the fans hate us so much, the fans actually threw up on our car.'"

"The cop had some mercy for us and let us go, but that's not the last time we got into some trouble on the road. There was this other time where Val Venis was driving, Test was in the passenger seat, and Prince Albert was in the back. We had this road rivalry where we were always throwing things at each other's cars as we drove, like water bottles or even eggs. But this one time, Val Venis drives up alongside us, and he tells me to pull over, yelling out to us that our car had a flat. We knew he was bullshitting us, but we pull over just in case. As I'm about to roll the window down, I see a flicker of light. Test had taken a shit in a bag and he was trying to light it and throw it into our car. But when Test tried to take a shit into the bag, he missed and shit all over his seat. So Prince Albert was dry-heaving in the back, which kind of gave things away. As soon as I saw the bag being lit, I screamed at Rodney to hit it, and we rolled up the window and took off. The bag of shit hit the trunk of our car, but we were just fast enough where I avoided getting hit in the face by a flying bag of shit on fire."

Pete Gas: "Back in late 2000, we were on a plane headed to Connecticut. Rodney and I were sitting in the front row of coach, and sitting in first class were Shane and Vince. We were sleeping when all of a sudden Rodney gets hit in the face with a magazine. Of course, it was Shane, because Shane would initiate shit all the time. So Rodney wants to throw it back, but Shane is ducking behind the big seat in first class while at the same time Shane is pointing to his dad, and Vince is asleep next to him. So Rodney flips Shane off and tries to go back to sleep, not wanting to do anything that would wake Vince up. But a couple of minutes later, Shane hits Rodney in the face again with another magazine. Shane starts laughing, and Vince wakes up, and now Vince realizes what's going on. So Rodney signals for the stewardess to come over. He has her make the announcement that wrestling Superstar Shane McMahon is on board the plane, and he'd be happy to sign autographs after the flight for all of his fans. All you could hear was this big chuckle from Vince. But Shane looks at us and he says, 'I'm getting even with you guys.' The following Monday night started a run of The Mean Street Posse versus The Acolytes where they basically beat the heck out of us for at least a month or two. The funny thing was it helped us in the long run because it helped us earn respect in the ring with the guys. But it wasn't too much fun while it was happening because they were out to see how tough we were, and they beat the shit out of us almost every night. That was Shane's revenge."

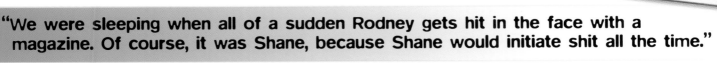

"We were sleeping when all of a sudden Rodney gets hit in the face with a magazine. Of course, it was Shane, because Shane would initiate shit all the time."

—Pete Gas

TRIPLE H ROAD STORY

Triple H: "When it came to invading Nitro, we sort of had a plan, but at the same time, we didn't have a plan. Luckily, there was the magic of editing because the first time I made my grand speech with the barrel of the gun sticking out from my crotch like a giant phallic reference, the gun actually didn't go off.

> ## "... The first time I made my grand speech with the barrel of the gun sticking out from my crotch like a giant phallic reference, the gun actually didn't go off."
>
> **—Triple H**

All you heard was a little poof and a few little things came out of the edges, so we had to shoot it a few times. If we could have done anything different, I would've tried to get in the building first. When we first showed up, they had no idea we were there, but by the time we did our promos in the parking lot, there was no chance we were getting in as they were making sure the arena was on lockdown. Eric Bischoff and the whole management crew at WCW would've been beyond pissed if we got in that building. I don't think that the boys from WCW would've started a legit fight with anybody, but my plan was to get inside and get inside the ring. If security or Bischoff touched me or threw a punch, I decided I was going to fall down and act like I just got hit in the head by an axe. I was going to scream so loud that it would cause a massive ball of confusion, enabling everyone else to grab the tapes and get out of there.

TRIPLE H ON THE ORIGINS OF THE ATTITUDE ERA

"The first time I ever heard of WWE moving out of the cartoon world and moving into the Attitude Era was in a meeting in Indianapolis toward the end of 1995 with The Kliq, Vince, and Gerald Brisco. Scott Hall and Kevin Nash had a beef with something going on, so Vince flew into Indianapolis to meet with them because he understood what they were saying about how the industry needed to evolve, but he wanted to hear more. I was new at the time and I went to the meeting just to say hello and leave. I didn't think it was my place, but when Vince saw me walk through the door, he wanted me to stay. So we all sat in that room, and everything that was discussed was a change in the way business was done and what needed to be done in order for the business to change. I'm not saying it was our idea and concept fully, but that was the first time I ever heard Vince talk about the Attitude Era and what it could be. I feel like that meeting was the spark that started it all."

"It's funny, because Lex Luger and Kevin Nash were running late to the arena that night, and when they rolled up, they saw us in the parking lot. Lex Luger stuck his head out the sunroof and was like, 'I think that's DX in a tank.' So when they went inside the building, they went into the production meeting and asked, 'Aren't you guys concerned about what's going on outside?' They had no idea we were out there in a tank. But when they found out, they freaked out and sent security to make sure all the doors were locked. If we would've went straight for the door, we would've gotten inside. Now that would've made for some great television. But we had a whole plan to continue the invasion.

"There was a secretary for WCW and Eric Bischoff who had just been let go, and a lot of the guys knew her because she worked in the office. So when she was let go, we ended up with all of Bischoff's travel itinerary for the next month. One of the things we were going to do is ambush him at the airport. This was before 9/11, and it didn't matter, you could grab a film crew and walk straight to the gate. So we were going to do that under the guise of journalism and ambush him with questions. But by that point, because of the invasion, we got into a whole cease and desist thing and we had to drop it. It would have been phenomenal if we could've pulled it off."